Singapore

LEVEL 2A

MATH

Appropriate for Students in **GRADE 3**

PRACTICE

Frank Schaffer
An imprint of Carson-Dellosa Publishing LLC
Greensboro, North Carolina

W9-BDF-475

Frank Schaffer
An imprint of Carson-Dellosa Publishing LLC
PO Box 35665
Greensboro, NC 27425 USA

Printed in the USA • All rights reserved.
01-295127784

ISBN 978-0-7682-3992-8

INTRODUCTION TO SINGAPORE MATH

Welcome to Singapore Math! The math curriculum in Singapore has been recognized worldwide for its excellence in producing students highly skilled in mathematics. Students in Singapore have ranked at the top in the world in mathematics on the *Trends in International Mathematics and Science Study* (TIMSS) in 1993, 1995, 2003, and 2008. Because of this, Singapore Math has gained in interest and popularity in the United States.

Singapore Math curriculum aims to help students develop the necessary math concepts and process skills for everyday life and to provide students with the ability to formulate, apply, and solve problems. Mathematics in the Singapore Primary (Elementary) Curriculum cover fewer topics but in greater depth. Key math concepts are introduced and built-on to reinforce various mathematical ideas and thinking. Students in Singapore are typically one grade level ahead of students in the United States.

The following pages provide examples of the various math problem types and skill sets taught in Singapore.

At an elementary level, some simple mathematical skills can help students understand mathematical principles. These skills are the counting-on, counting-back, and crossing-out methods. Note that these methods are most useful when the numbers are small.

1. The Counting-On Method

Used for addition of two numbers. Count on in 1s with the help of a picture or number line.

$$7 + 4 = \mathbf{11}$$

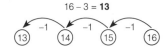

2. The Counting-Back Method

Used for subtraction of two numbers. Count back in 1s with the help of a picture or number line.

$$16 - 3 = \mathbf{13}$$

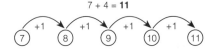

3. The Crossing-Out Method

Used for subtraction of two numbers. Cross out the number of items to be taken away. Count the remaining ones to find the answer.

$$20 - 12 = \mathbf{8}$$

A **number bond** shows the relationship in a simple addition or subtraction problem. The number bond is based on the concept "part-part-whole." This concept is useful in teaching simple addition and subtraction to young children.

To find a whole, students must add the two parts.
To find a part, students must subtract the other part from the whole.

The different types of number bonds are illustrated below.

1. Number Bond (single digits)

3 (part) + 6 (part) = **9** (whole)

9 (whole) − 3 (part) = **6** (part)

9 (whole) − 6 (part) = **3** (part)

2. Addition Number Bond (single digits)

= 9 + 1 + 4   Make a ten first.
= 10 + 4
= **14**

3. Addition Number Bond (double and single digits)

= 2 + 5 + 10   Regroup 15 into 5 and 10.
= 7 + 10
= **17**

4. Subtraction Number Bond (double and single digits)

10 − 7 = 3
3 + 2 = **5**

5. Subtraction Number Bond (double digits)

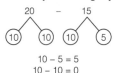

10 − 5 = 5
10 − 10 = 0
5 + 0 = **5**

Students should understand that multiplication is repeated addition and that division is the grouping of all items into equal sets.

1. Repeated Addition (Multiplication)

Mackenzie eats 2 rolls a day. How many rolls does she eat in 5 days?

$$2 + 2 + 2 + 2 + 2 = 10$$
$$5 \times 2 = 10$$

She eats **10** rolls in 5 days.

2. The Grouping Method (Division)

Mrs. Lee makes 14 sandwiches. She gives all the sandwiches equally to 7 friends. How many sandwiches does each friend receive?

$$14 \div 7 = 2$$

Each friend receives **2** sandwiches.

One of the basic but essential math skills students should acquire is to perform the 4 operations of whole numbers and fractions. Each of these methods is illustrated below.

1. The Adding-Without-Regrouping Method

```
  H T O
  3 2 1          O: Ones
+ 5 6 8          T: Tens
-------
  8 8 9          H: Hundreds
```

Since no regrouping is required, add the digits in each place value accordingly.

2. The Adding-by-Regrouping Method

```
  H T O
  ¹4 9 2         O: Ones
+ 1 5 3          T: Tens
-------
  6 4 5          H: Hundreds
```

In this example, regroup 14 tens into 1 hundred 4 tens.

Singapore Math Practice Level 2A

3. The Adding-by-Regrouping-Twice Method

$$
\begin{array}{c}
\text{H}\ \text{T}\ \text{O} \\
{}^{1}2\ {}^{1}8\ 6 \\
+\ 3\ 6\ 5 \\
\hline
6\ 5\ 1
\end{array}
$$

O: Ones
T: Tens
H: Hundreds

Regroup twice in this example.
First, regroup 11 ones into 1 ten 1 one.
Second, regroup 15 tens into 1 hundred 5 tens.

4. The Subtracting-Without-Regrouping Method

$$
\begin{array}{c}
\text{H}\ \text{T}\ \text{O} \\
7\ 3\ 9 \\
-\ 3\ 2\ 5 \\
\hline
4\ 1\ 4
\end{array}
$$

O: Ones
T: Tens
H: Hundreds

Since no regrouping is required, subtract the digits in each place value accordingly.

5. The Subtracting-by-Regrouping Method

$$
\begin{array}{c}
\text{H}\ \text{T}\ \text{O} \\
5\ {}^{7}8\ {}^{11}1 \\
-\ 2\ 4\ 7 \\
\hline
3\ 3\ 4
\end{array}
$$

O: Ones
T: Tens
H: Hundreds

In this example, students cannot subtract 7 ones from 1 one. So, regroup the tens and ones. Regroup 8 tens 1 one into 7 tens 11 ones.

6. The Subtracting-by-Regrouping-Twice Method

$$
\begin{array}{c}
\text{H}\ \text{T}\ \text{O} \\
{}^{7}8\ {}^{9}0\ {}^{10}0 \\
-\ 5\ 9\ 3 \\
\hline
2\ 0\ 7
\end{array}
$$

O: Ones
T: Tens
H: Hundreds

In this example, students cannot subtract 3 ones from 0 ones and 9 tens from 0 tens. So, regroup the hundreds, tens, and ones. Regroup 8 hundreds into 7 hundreds 9 tens 10 ones.

7. The Multiplying-Without-Regrouping Method

$$
\begin{array}{c}
\text{T}\ \text{O} \\
2\ 4 \\
\times\ \ \ 2 \\
\hline
4\ 8
\end{array}
$$

O: Ones
T: Tens

Since no regrouping is required, multiply the digit in each place value by the multiplier accordingly.

8. The Multiplying-With-Regrouping Method

$$
\begin{array}{c}
\text{H}\ \text{T}\ \text{O} \\
{}^{1}3\ {}^{2}4\ 9 \\
\times\ \ \ \ \ 3 \\
\hline
1,0\ 4\ 7
\end{array}
$$

O: Ones
T: Tens
H: Hundreds

In this example, regroup 27 ones into 2 tens 7 ones, and 14 tens into 1 hundred 4 tens.

9. The Dividing-Without-Regrouping Method

$$
\begin{array}{r}
2\ 4\ 1 \\
2{\overline{\smash{\big)}\,4\ 8\ 2}} \\
\underline{-4} \\
8 \\
\underline{-8} \\
2 \\
\underline{-2} \\
0
\end{array}
$$

Since no regrouping is required, divide the digit in each place value by the divisor accordingly.

10. The Dividing-With-Regrouping Method

$$
\begin{array}{r}
1\ 6\ 6 \\
5{\overline{\smash{\big)}\,8\ 3\ 0}} \\
\underline{-5} \\
3\ 3 \\
\underline{-3\ 0} \\
3\ 0 \\
\underline{-3\ 0} \\
0
\end{array}
$$

In this example, regroup 3 hundreds into 30 tens and add 3 tens to make 33 tens. Regroup 3 tens into 30 ones.

11. The Addition-of-Fractions Method

$$
\frac{1 \times 2}{6 \times 2} + \frac{1 \times 3}{4 \times 3} = \frac{2}{12} + \frac{3}{12} = \frac{5}{12}
$$

Always remember to make the denominators common before adding the fractions.

12. The Subtraction-of-Fractions Method

$$
\frac{1 \times 5}{2 \times 5} - \frac{1 \times 2}{5 \times 2} = \frac{5}{10} - \frac{2}{10} = \frac{3}{10}
$$

Always remembers to make the denominators common before subtracting the fractions.

13. The Multiplication-of-Fractions Method

$$
\frac{{}^{1}\cancel{3}}{5} \times \frac{1}{\cancel{3}_{3}} = \frac{1}{15}
$$

When the numerator and the denominator have a common multiple, reduce them to their lowest fractions.

14. The Division-of-Fractions Method

$$
\frac{7}{9} \div \frac{1}{6} = \frac{7}{\cancel{9}_{3}} \times \frac{\cancel{6}^{2}}{1} = \frac{14}{3} = 4\frac{2}{3}
$$

When dividing fractions, first change the division sign (÷) to the multiplication sign (×). Then, switch the numerator and denominator of the fraction on the right hand side. Multiply the fractions in the usual way.

Model drawing is an effective strategy used to solve math word problems. It is a visual representation of the information in word problems using bar units. By drawing the models, students will know of the variables given in the problem, the variables to find, and even the methods used to solve the problem.

Drawing models is also a versatile strategy. It can be applied to simple word problems involving addition, subtraction, multiplication, and division. It can also be applied to word problems related to fractions, decimals, percentage, and ratio.

The use of models also trains students to think in an algebraic manner, which uses symbols for representation.

The different types of bar models used to solve word problems are illustrated below.

1. The model that involves addition

Melissa has 50 blue beads and 20 red beads. How many beads does she have altogether?

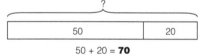

$$50 + 20 = \mathbf{70}$$

2. The model that involves subtraction

Ben and Andy have 90 toy cars. Andy has 60 toy cars. How many toy cars does Ben have?

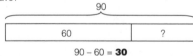

$$90 - 60 = \mathbf{30}$$

3. The model that involves comparison

Mr. Simons has 150 magazines and 110 books in his study. How many more magazines than books does he have?

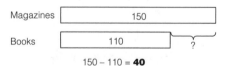

$$150 - 110 = \mathbf{40}$$

4. The model that involves two items with a difference

A pair of shoes costs $109. A leather bag costs $241 more than the pair of shoes. How much is the leather bag?

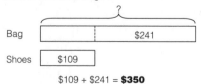

$$\$109 + \$241 = \mathbf{\$350}$$

4

5. The model that involves multiples

Mrs. Drew buys 12 apples. She buys 3 times as many oranges as apples. She also buys 3 times as many cherries as oranges. How many pieces of fruit does she buy altogether?

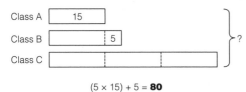

$$13 \times 12 = \textbf{156}$$

6. The model that involves multiples and difference

There are 15 students in Class A. There are 5 more students in Class B than in Class A. There are 3 times as many students in Class C than in Class A. How many students are there altogether in the three classes?

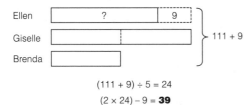

$$(5 \times 15) + 5 = \textbf{80}$$

7. The model that involves creating a whole

Ellen, Giselle, and Brenda bake 111 muffins. Giselle bakes twice as many muffins as Brenda. Ellen bakes 9 fewer muffins than Giselle. How many muffins does Ellen bake?

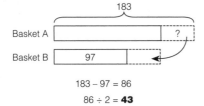

$$(111 + 9) \div 5 = 24$$
$$(2 \times 24) - 9 = \textbf{39}$$

8. The model that involves sharing

There are 183 tennis balls in Basket A and 97 tennis balls in Basket B. How many tennis balls must be transferred from Basket A to Basket B so that both baskets contain the same number of tennis balls?

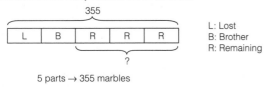

$$183 - 97 = 86$$
$$86 \div 2 = \textbf{43}$$

9. The model that involves fractions

George had 355 marbles. He lost $\frac{1}{5}$ of the marbles and gave $\frac{1}{4}$ of the remaining marbles to his brother. How many marbles did he have left?

355

| L | B | R | R | R |

L: Lost
B: Brother
R: Remaining

?

5 parts → 355 marbles
1 part → 355 ÷ 5 = 71 marbles
3 parts → 3 × 71 = **213** marbles

10. The model that involves ratio

Aaron buys a tie and a belt. The prices of the tie and belt are in the ratio 2 : 5. If both items cost $539,

(a) what is the price of the tie?

(b) what is the price of the belt?

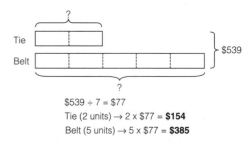

$$\$539 \div 7 = \$77$$
Tie (2 units) → 2 × $77 = **$154**
Belt (5 units) → 5 × $77 = **$385**

11. The model that involves comparison of fractions

Jack's height is $\frac{2}{3}$ of Leslie's height. Leslie's height is $\frac{3}{4}$ of Lindsay's height. If Lindsay is 160 cm tall, find Jack's height and Leslie's height.

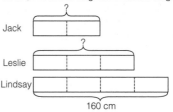

160 cm

1 unit → 160 ÷ 4 = 40 cm

Leslie's height (3 units) → 3 × 40 = **120 cm**

Jack's height (2 units) → 2 × 40 = **80 cm**

Thinking skills and strategies are important in mathematical problem solving. These skills are applied when students think through the math problems to solve them. Below are some commonly used thinking skills and strategies applied in mathematical problem solving.

1. Comparing

Comparing is a form of thinking skill that students can apply to identify similarities and differences.

When comparing numbers, look carefully at each digit before deciding if a number is greater or less than the other. Students might also use a number line for comparison when there are more numbers.

Example:

3 is greater than 2 but smaller than 7.

2. Sequencing

A sequence shows the order of a series of numbers. *Sequencing* is a form of thinking skill that requires students to place numbers in a particular order. There are many terms in a sequence. The terms refer to the numbers in a sequence.

To place numbers in a correct order, students must first find a rule that generates the sequence. In a simple math sequence, students can either add or subtract to find the unknown terms in the sequence.

Example: Find the 7th term in the sequence below.

1,	4,	7,	10,	13,	16	?
1st term	2nd term	3rd term	4th term	5th term	6th term	7th term

Step 1: This sequence is in an increasing order.

Step 2: 4 − 1 = 3   7 − 4 = 3
The difference between two consecutive terms is 3.

Step 3: 16 + 3 = 19
The 7th term is **19**.

3. Visualization

Visualization is a problem solving strategy that can help students visualize a problem through the use of physical objects. Students will play a more active role in solving the problem by manipulating these objects.

The main advantage of using this strategy is the mobility of information in the process of solving the problem. When students make a wrong step in the process, they can retrace the step without erasing or canceling it.

The other advantage is that this strategy helps develop a better understanding of the problem or solution through visual objects or images. In this way, students will be better able to remember how to solve these types of problems.

Some of the commonly used objects for this strategy are toothpicks, straws, cards, strings, water, sand, pencils, paper, and dice.

4. Look for a Pattern

This strategy requires the use of observational and analytical skills. Students have to observe the given data to find a pattern in order to solve the problem. Math word problems that involve the use of this strategy usually have repeated numbers or patterns.

Example: Find the sum of all the numbers from 1 to 100.

Step 1: Simplify the problem.
Find the sum of 1, 2, 3, 4, 5, 6, 7, 8, 9, and 10.

Step 2: Look for a pattern.

$1 + 10 = 11$ $2 + 9 = 11$ $3 + 8 = 11$
$4 + 7 = 11$ $5 + 6 = 11$

Step 3: Describe the pattern.
When finding the sum of 1 to 10, add the first and last numbers to get a result of 11. Then, add the second and second last numbers to get the same result. The pattern continues until all the numbers from 1 to 10 are added. There will be 5 pairs of such results. Since each addition equals 11, the answer is then $5 \times 11 = 55$.

Step 4: Use the pattern to find the answer.
Since there are 5 pairs in the sum of 1 to 10, there should be ($10 \times 5 = 50$ pairs) in the sum of 1 to 100.

Note that the addition for each pair is not equal to 11 now. The addition for each pair is now ($1 + 100 = 101$).

$$50 \times 101 = 5050$$

The sum of all the numbers from 1 to 100 is **5,050**.

5. Working Backward

The strategy of working backward applies only to a specific type of math word problem. These word problems state the end result, and students are required to find the total number. In order to solve these word problems, students have to work backward by thinking through the correct sequence of events. The strategy of working backward allows students to use their logical reasoning and sequencing to find the answers.

Example: Sarah has a piece of ribbon. She cuts the ribbon into 4 equal parts. Each part is then cut into 3 smaller equal parts. If the length of each small part is 35 cm, how long is the piece of ribbon?

$$3 \times 35 = 105 \text{ cm}$$
$$4 \times 105 = 420 \text{ cm}$$

The piece of ribbon is **420 cm**.

6. The Before-After Concept

The *Before-After* concept lists all the relevant data before and after an event. Students can then compare the differences and eventually solve the problems. Usually, the Before-After concept and the mathematical model go hand in hand to solve math word problems. Note that the Before-After concept can be applied only to a certain type of math word problem, which trains students to think sequentially.

Example: Kelly has 4 times as much money as Joey. After Kelly uses some money to buy a tennis racquet, and Joey uses $30 to buy a pair of pants, Kelly has twice as much money as Joey. If Joey has $98 in the beginning,
(a) how much money does Kelly have in the end?
(b) how much money does Kelly spend on the tennis racquet?

Before

Kelly

Joey $98

After

Kelly

Joey $30

(a) $98 - $30 = $68
2 × $68 = $136
Kelly has **$136** in the end.

(b) 4 × $98 = $392
$392 - $136 = $256
Kelly spends **$256** on the tennis racquet.

7. Making Supposition

Making supposition is commonly known as "making an assumption." Students can use this strategy to solve certain types of math word problems. Making assumptions will eliminate some possibilities and simplifies the word problems by providing a boundary of values to work within.

Example: Mrs. Jackson bought 100 pieces of candy for all the students in her class. How many pieces of candy would each student receive if there were 25 students in her class?

In the above word problem, assume that each student received the same number of pieces. This eliminates the possibilities that some students would receive more than others due to good behaviour, better results, or any other reason.

8. Representation of Problem

In problem solving, students often use representations in the solutions to show their understanding of the problems. Using representations also allow students to understand the mathematical concepts and relationships as well as to manipulate the information presented in the problems. Examples of representations are diagrams and lists or tables.

Diagrams allow students to consolidate or organize the information given in the problems. By drawing a diagram, students can see the problem clearly and solve it effectively.

A list or table can help students organize information that is useful for analysis. After analyzing, students can then see a pattern, which can be used to solve the problem.

9. Guess and Check

One of the most important and effective problem-solving techniques is *Guess and Check*. It is also known as *Trial and Error*. As the name suggests, students have to guess the answer to a problem and check if that guess is correct. If the guess is wrong, students will make another guess. This will continue until the guess is correct.

It is beneficial to keep a record of all the guesses and checks in a table. In addition, a *Comments* column can be included. This will enable students to analyze their guess (if it is too high or too low) and improve on the next guess. Be careful; this problem-solving technique can be tiresome without systematic or logical guesses.

Example: Jessica had 15 coins. Some of them were 10-cent coins and the rest were 5-cent coins. The total amount added up to $1.25. How many coins of each kind were there?

Use the guess-and-check method.

Number of 10¢ Coins	Value	Number of 5¢ Coins	Value	Total Number of Coins	Total Value
7	$7 \times 10¢ = 70¢$	8	$8 \times 5¢ = 40¢$	$7 + 8 = 15$	70¢ + 40¢ = 110¢ = $1.10
8	$8 \times 10¢ = 80¢$	7	$7 \times 5¢ = 35¢$	$8 + 7 = 15$	80¢ + 35¢ = 115¢ = $1.15
10	$10 \times 10¢ = 100¢$	5	$5 \times 5¢ = 25¢$	$10 + 5 = 15$	100¢ + 25¢ = 125¢ = $1.25

There were **ten** 10-cent coins and **five** 5-cent coins.

10. Restate the Problem

When solving challenging math problems, conventional methods may not be workable. Instead, restating the problem will enable students to see some challenging problems in a different light so that they can better understand them.

The strategy of restating the problem is to "say" the problem in a different and clearer way. However, students have to ensure that the main idea of the problem is not altered.

How do students restate a math problem?

First, read and understand the problem. Gather the given facts and unknowns. Note any condition(s) that have to be satisfied.

Next, restate the problem. Imagine narrating this problem to a friend. Present the given facts, unknown(s), and condition(s). Students may want to write the "revised" problem. Once the "revised" problem is analyzed, students should be able to think of an appropriate strategy to solve it.

11. Simplify the Problem

One of the commonly used strategies in mathematical problem solving is simplification of the problem. When a problem is simplified, it can be "broken down" into two or more smaller parts. Students can then solve the parts systematically to get to the final answer.

Singapore Math Practice Level 2A

Table of Contents

LEARNING OUTCOMES

Unit 1 Numbers 1-1,000
Students should be able to
- recognize and write numbers up to 1,000 in numerals and words.
- identify the place value of numbers up to 1,000.
- compare and arrange numbers up to 1,000.
- complete number patterns.

Unit 2 Adding and Subtracting Numbers 1-1,000
Students should be able to
- add and subtract numbers up to 1,000 by regrouping ones, tens, or hundreds.
- solve 1-step story problems related to addition and subtraction.

Review 1
This review tests students' understanding of Units 1 & 2.

Unit 3 Fun With Models (Adding and Subtracting)
Students should be able to
- draw models involving addition and subtraction of 2 numbers.
- draw models involving addition of 3 numbers.

Unit 4 Multiplying and Dividing
Students should be able to
- multiply numbers by 2, 3, 4, 5, and 10.
- divide numbers by 2, 3, 4, 5, and 10.

Review 2
This review tests students' understanding of Units 3 & 4.

Unit 5 Multiplying and Dividing Numbers by 2 and 3
Students should be able to
- multiply and divide numbers by 2 and 3.

Unit 6 Multiplying and Dividing Numbers by 4, 5, and 10
Students should be able to
- multiply numbers by 4, 5, and 10.
- divide numbers by 4, 5, and 10.
- solve 1-step multiplication and division story problems.

Unit 7 Fun With Models (Multiplying and Dividing)
Students should be able to
- draw models involving multiplication and division.

Review 3
This review tests students' understanding of Units 5, 6, & 7.

Unit 8 Length
Students should be able to
- measure objects in meters, centimeters, inches, feet, and yards.
- compare items of different lengths.
- add, subtract, multiply, and divide different lengths.
- solve 1-step story problems related to length.

Unit 9 Mass
Students should be able to
- measure items in kilograms, grams, ounces, and pounds.
- compare items of different masses.
- add, subtract, multiply, and divide different masses.
- solve 1-step story problems related to mass.

Review 4
This review tests students' understanding of Units 8 & 9.

Final Review
This review is an excellent assessment of students' understanding of all the topics in this book.

Singapore Math Practice Level 2A

FORMULA SHEET

Unit 1 Numbers 1-1,000

Numbers can be written as words.
Example: 549 **five hundred and forty-nine**

Place value

The value of a digit is based on its place value in the number.
Examples: In 637,

        the digit **7** is in the **ones** place,
        the digit **3** is in the **tens** place, and
        the digit **6** is in the **hundreds** place.

Comparing numbers

Use the place value starting with hundreds to compare 2 numbers.
- When one number is bigger than the other, use the words *greater than* to describe it.
- When one number is less than the other, use the words *smaller than* to describe it.

Order and Pattern

When arranging a set of numbers in order,
- determine if the series must begin with the largest or the smallest,
- compare the place value of the numbers,
- arrange the numbers in the correct order.

For number pattern problems,
- determine if the number pattern is in an increasing or a decreasing order,
- find the difference between 2 consecutive numbers,
- apply the difference to find the unknown number.

Unit 2 Adding and Subtracting Numbers 1-1,000

Adding without regrouping

- Add the digits in the ones place first.
- Add the digits in the tens place.
- Add the digits in the hundreds place.

Adding with regrouping

- Add the digits in the ones place first. Regroup the ones if there are more than 10 ones.
- Add the digits in the tens place. Add another ten if there is a regrouping of ones. Regroup the tens if there are more than 10 tens.
- Add the digits in the hundreds place. Add another hundred if there is a regrouping of tens.

Subtracting without regrouping

- Subtract the digits in the ones place first.
- Subtract the digits in the tens place.
- Subtract the digits in the hundreds place.

Subtracting with regrouping

- Subtract the digits in the ones place first. If this is not possible, regroup the tens and ones.
- Subtract the digits in the tens place. If this is not possible, regroup the hundreds and tens.
- Subtract the digits in the hundreds place.

Unit 3 Fun With Models (Adding and Subtracting)

Models are pictorial representations of mathematical problems. Models make the problems easier to understand and solve.

The following is an example of a model involving simple addition.

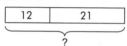

The following is an example of a model involving addition of 3 items.

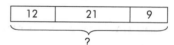

The following is an example of a model involving simple subtraction.

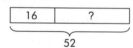

The following is an example of a model involving comparing.

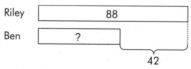

The following is an example of a model in a 2-part story problem.

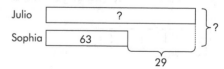

Singapore Math Practice Level 2A

Unit 4 Multiplying and Dividing

Multiplication is also known as repeated addition.

Keywords: *times*, *multiply*, or *product*

For example, $4 \times 5 = 4 + 4 + 4 + 4 + 4$

$$
\underset{\substack{\text{(number)}}}{4} \quad \underset{\substack{\text{(number} \\ \text{of times)}}}{\times \quad 5} \quad \underset{\substack{\text{(result)}}}{= \quad 20}
$$

Division is the opposite of multiplication.

Keywords: *equal*, *equally*, or *divide*

The ÷ sign is used to represent division in a number sentence.

Examples: $20 \div 4 = 5$ or $20 \div 5 = 4$

Unit 5 Multiplying and Dividing Numbers by 2 and 3

Below are the multiplication tables of 2 and 3.

×	2	3
1	2	3
2	4	6
3	6	9
4	8	12
5	10	15
6	12	18
7	14	21
8	16	24
9	18	27
10	20	30
11	22	33
12	24	36

Unit 6 Multiplying and Dividing Numbers by 4, 5, and 10

Below are the multiplication tables of 4, 5, and 10.

×	4	5	10
1	4	5	10
2	8	10	20
3	12	15	30
4	16	20	40
5	20	25	50
6	24	30	60
7	28	35	70
8	32	40	80
9	36	45	90
10	40	50	100
11	44	55	110
12	48	60	120

Unit 7 Fun With Models (Multiplying and Dividing)

The following is an example of a model involving simple multiplication.

The following are examples of a model involving simple division.

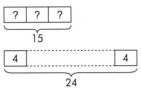

Unit 8 Length

Length is how long an object is.
Height is how tall an object is.

Units of measurement are meters (m), centimeters (cm), inches (in.), feet (ft.), and yards (yd.).

When measuring the length of an object with a ruler, always place the object starting at the 0 on the ruler. If the starting point of the object is not at 0, subtract the markings on both ends of the object to find the actual length of the object.

<u>4 operations of length</u>

When adding, subtracting, multiplying, and dividing lengths, make sure that they are in the same unit of measurement.

Unit 9 Mass

Mass is how heavy an object is.

Units of measurement are kilograms (kg), grams (g), ounces (oz.), and pounds (lb.).

<u>Comparing the mass of 2 objects</u>

When 2 objects have the same mass, use the words *as heavy as*.

When the mass of one object is heavier than that of the other object, use the words *more than*.

When the mass of one object is lighter than that of the other object, use the words *less than*.

<u>Reading the mass of an object using a scale</u>

When the object is placed on a scale, the needle will move and point to a number. That number is the mass of the object. Note the unit of measurement on the scale.

<u>4 operations of mass</u>

When adding, subtracting, multiplying, and dividing masses, make sure that they are in the same unit of measurement.

Unit 1: NUMBERS 1–1,000

Examples:

1. Write 909 in words.   <u>nine hundred and nine</u>

2. In 285, which digit is in the tens place?   <u>8</u>

3. In 704, in which place is the digit 4?   <u>ones</u>

4. Fill in the blank with *greater* or *smaller*.

   530 is _____ than 503.   <u>greater</u>

5. 50 less than 955 is _____.   <u>905</u>

6. Fill in the missing numbers in the number pattern.

   410, 430, _____, _____, 490, 510   <u>450, 470</u>

Count the squares, and write the correct numbers on the lines.

1.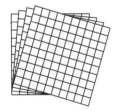

   _____

2.

   _____

Singapore Math Practice Level 2A

3.

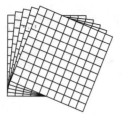

_____

4.

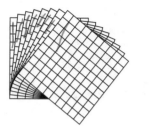

_____

5.

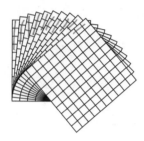

_____

Write the following numbers as words on the lines.

6. 760 _____

7. 378 _____

8. 456 _____

9. 202 _____

10. 1,000 _____

Write the numbers on the lines.

11. five hundred and sixty-two   _____

12. seven hundred and seventy-nine   _____

13. one hundred and ten   _____

14

14. three hundred and fifty-eight _____

15. nine hundred and seven _____

Fill in each blank with the correct answer.

16. 825 = _____ hundreds _____ tens _____ ones

17. 630 = _____ hundreds _____ tens _____ ones

18. 705 = _____ hundreds _____ tens _____ ones

19. 459 = _____ hundreds _____ tens _____ ones

20. 1,000 = _____ hundreds _____ tens _____ ones

21. In 671, the digit 7 is in the _____ place.

22. In 415, the digit 4 is in the _____ place.

23. In 567, the digit 5 is in the _____ place.

24. In 928, the digit _____ is in the hundreds place.

25. In 873, the digit _____ is in the ones place.

26. In 609, the digit _____ is in the tens place.

Fill in each blank with *smaller* or *greater*.

27. 400 is _____ than 40.

28. 926 is _____ than 962.

29. 370 is _____ than 730.

30. 805 is _____ than 580.

31. 235 is _____ than 352.

15

Singapore Math Practice Level 2A

Arrange these numbers in order. Begin with the smallest.

32.　397　379　973　937

_____

33.　192　129　319　219

_____

34.　715　571　751　511

_____

35.　163　116　316　313

_____

36.　404　434　443　344

_____

Arrange these numbers in order. Begin with the largest.

37.　570　705　507　750

_____

38.　314　413　134　341

_____

Singapore Math Practice Level 2A

39. | 289 | 960 | 187 | 517 | 608 |

_____

40. | 320 | 190 | 857 | 220 | 456 |

_____

41. | 927 | 279 | 727 | 970 | 290 |

_____

Fill in each blank with the correct answer.

42. 10 more than 560 is _____.

43. 20 less than 680 is _____.

44. _____ is 100 more than 778.

45. _____ is 200 less than 695.

46. _____ is 5 less than 279.

Complete the number patterns.

47. 280, 290, _____, _____, 320

48. 970, 870, 770, _____, _____

49. 760, _____, 800, 820, _____

50. 430, 460, _____, _____, 550

51. _____, _____, 650, 750, 850

Singapore Math Practice Level 2A

Unit 2: ADDING AND SUBTRACTING NUMBERS 1–1,000

Examples:

1.
```
   3 1 6
 + 1 2 1
   4 3 7
```

2.
```
   6 2 5
 − 3 1 3
   3 1 2
```

3.
```
   ¹ ¹
   4 8 3
 + 3 9 8
   8 8 1
```

4.
```
   ⁶ ⁹ ¹⁰
   7̶ 0̶ 0̶
 − 2 9 3
   4 0 7
```

Solve the addition problems below.

1.
```
   1 4 3
 + 2 1 4
```

2.
```
   3 1 2
 + 4 8 1
```

3.
```
   7 3 2
 + 1 4 5
```

4.
```
   2 0 1
 + 2 8 3
```

5.
```
   8 2 1
 + 1 6 3
```

Solve the subtraction problems below.

6.
```
   5 6 9
 − 2 3 4
```

7.
```
   9 3 2
 − 1 2 1
```

Singapore Math Practice Level 2A

8.
$$
\begin{array}{r}
7\,3\,6 \\
-\ 2\,0\,4 \\
\hline
\end{array}
$$

10.
$$
\begin{array}{r}
8\,5\,9 \\
-\ 6\,0\,7 \\
\hline
\end{array}
$$

9.
$$
\begin{array}{r}
3\,7\,5 \\
-\ 1\,5\,2 \\
\hline
\end{array}
$$

Solve the following addition problems by regrouping.

11.
$$
\begin{array}{r}
1\,3\,5 \\
+\,1\,0\,9 \\
\hline
\end{array}
$$

14.
$$
\begin{array}{r}
2\,5\,6 \\
+\,3\,8\,0 \\
\hline
\end{array}
$$

12.
$$
\begin{array}{r}
5\,0\,5 \\
+\,2\,9\,5 \\
\hline
\end{array}
$$

15.
$$
\begin{array}{r}
4\,6\,2 \\
+\,2\,0\,8 \\
\hline
\end{array}
$$

13.
$$
\begin{array}{r}
7\,3\,7 \\
+\,1\,2\,9 \\
\hline
\end{array}
$$

16.
$$
\begin{array}{r}
3\,9\,7 \\
+\,5\,4\,6 \\
\hline
\end{array}
$$

Solve the following subtraction problems by regrouping.

17.
$$
\begin{array}{r}
3\,5\,3 \\
-\,1\,7\,4 \\
\hline
\end{array}
$$

20.
$$
\begin{array}{r}
6\,3\,2 \\
-\,1\,7\,1 \\
\hline
\end{array}
$$

18.
$$
\begin{array}{r}
9\,7\,1 \\
-\,3\,6\,9 \\
\hline
\end{array}
$$

21.
$$
\begin{array}{r}
4\,1\,2 \\
-\,1\,2\,4 \\
\hline
\end{array}
$$

19.
$$
\begin{array}{r}
4\,0\,0 \\
-\,2\,0\,5 \\
\hline
\end{array}
$$

22.
$$
\begin{array}{r}
5\,0\,0 \\
-\,1\,7\,8 \\
\hline
\end{array}
$$

Singapore Math Practice Level 2A

23.
```
   8 0 0
 − 2 8 0
 ─────
```

24.
```
   9 8 0
 − 5 5 5
 ─────
```

25. Match each balloon to the correct tag.

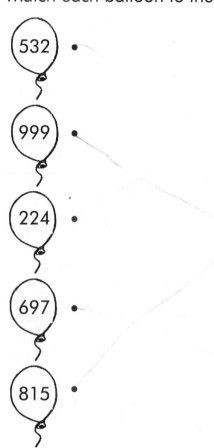

(532) •

(999) •

(224) •

(697) •

(815) •

• 🎀 592 − 368

• 🎀 446 + 369

• 🎀 1,000 − 468

• 🎀 319 + 680

• 🎀 856 − 159

Fill in each empty box with a +, − or = sign.

26.

73		42		115
70		30		40
3	+	72		75

27.

231		124		355
115		96		19
116		220		336

Singapore Math Practice Level 2A

Solve the following story problems. Show your work in the space below.

28. Lena collects 389 stickers. Anne collects 317 more stickers than Lena. How many stickers does Anne collect?

Anne collects _____ stickers.

29. Tom has 416 bottle caps. John has 29 bottle caps fewer than Tom. How many bottle caps does John have?

John has _____ bottle caps.

30. Mr. Abdul sold 586 roses on Monday. He sold 237 roses on Tuesday. How many roses did he sell altogether?

He sold _____ roses altogether.

Singapore Math Practice Level 2A

31. There were 416 visitors to a museum on Saturday. There were 555 visitors to the museum on Sunday. How many visitors were at the museum on both days?

_____ visitors were at the museum on both days.

32. Marcus and Jack spent $837 at a computer fair. If Jack spent $469, how much did Marcus spend?

Marcus spent $_____.

Singapore Math Practice Level 2A

REVIEW 1

Write the following numbers as words on the lines.

1. 375 _____

2. 919 _____

Write the numbers on the lines.

3. two hundred and twelve   _____

4. three hundred and three   _____

5. Arrange these numbers in order. Begin with the largest.

| 313 | 420 | 179 | 402 | 917 |

_____ , _____ , _____ , _____ , _____

6. Arrange these numbers in order. Begin with the smallest.

| 812 | 128 | 182 | 281 | 218 |

_____ , _____ , _____ , _____ , _____

Fill in each blank with the correct answer.

7. 10 more than 360 is _____.

8. 50 less than 876 is _____.

9. 536, _____, 496, 476, _____

Singapore Math Practice Level 2A

Solve the problems below. Show your work.

10.
```
   608
 + 129
 ─────
```

11.
```
   576
 + 188
 ─────
```

12.
```
   154
 + 365
 ─────
```

13.
```
   312
 + 498
 ─────
```

14.
```
   700
 - 435
 ─────
```

15.
```
   328
 - 109
 ─────
```

16.
```
   860
 - 389
 ─────
```

17.
```
   542
 - 379
 ─────
```

Solve the following story problems. Show your work in the space below.

18. The table below shows the number of people who went to the zoo on 3 different days.

Monday	Tuesday	Wednesday
379	686	575

(a) How many more people went to the zoo on Wednesday than on Monday?

_____ more people went to the zoo on Wednesday than on Monday.

Singapore Math Practice Level 2A

(b)   How many fewer people went to the zoo on Monday than on Tuesday?

_____ fewer people went to the zoo on Monday than on Tuesday.

19.   Aaron has collected 494 stamps. He wants to collect 1,000 stamps. How many more stamps does Aaron need to collect?

Aaran needs to collect _____ more stamps.

20.   Jazmin sold 360 flowers on Friday. She sold 265 flowers on Saturday. How many flowers did Jazmin sell on both days?

Jazmin sold _____ flowers on both days.

Singapore Math Practice Level 2A

Unit 3: FUN WITH MODELS (ADDING AND SUBTRACTING)

Examples:

1. James has 93 postcards.

    Anya has 62 postcards.

    How many postcards do they have altogether?

    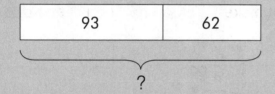

    $$93 + 62 = 155$$

    They have **155** postcards altogether.

2. Aunt Lily had $59.

    She spent $17 on a book.

    How much did she have left?

$17	?

    $59

    $$\$59 - \$17 = \$42$$

    She had **$42** left.

Draw the models, and solve the following story problems.

1. Danny has 576 bookmarks. Emilio has 186 bookmarks. How many bookmarks do they have altogether?

They have _____ bookmarks altogether.

2. Eddy has 280 chickens. He sells 168 chickens. How many chickens does he have left?

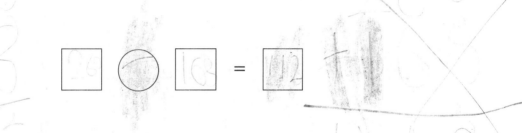

He has _____ chickens left.

3. A shopkeeper sold 360 oranges on Monday. He sold 275 oranges on Tuesday and another 150 oranges on Wednesday. How many oranges did he sell altogether?

He sold _____ oranges altogether.

Singapore Math Practice Level 2A

4. Samantha had 96 seashells. She gave some to her best friend. She had 78 seashells left. How many did she give to her best friend?

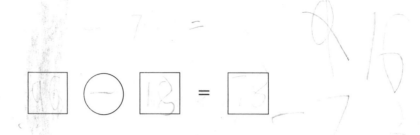

She gave _____ seashells to her best friend.

5. Andy received 131 stamps from his father. His sister gave him 280 stamps. How many stamps did he have altogether?

He had _____ stamps altogether.

6. There are 216 chickens, 137 ducks, and 97 rabbits on a farm. How many animals are there on the farm?

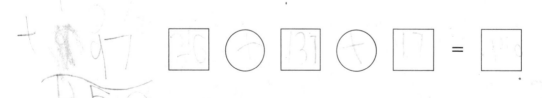

There are _____ animals on the farm.

Singapore Math Practice Level 2A

7. Malik had 720 trading cards. He gave some to his brother. He had 465 trading cards left. How many trading cards did he give to his brother?

He gave _____ trading cards to his brother.

8. Hitomi saves $310. Her brother saves $280 more than Hitomi.

(a) How much does her brother save?

Her brother saves $_____.

(b) How much do they save altogether?

They save $_____ altogether.

Unit 4: MULTIPLYING AND DIVIDING

Examples:

1.

There are 5 plates on a table.

There are 2 crackers on each plate.

How many crackers are there altogether?

$$5 \times 2 = 10$$

There are <u>10</u> crackers altogether.

2.

Natalie bought 16 ears of sweet corn.

She put an equal number of ears of corn into 4 bags.

How many ears of corn are there in each bag?

$$16 \div 4 = 4$$

There are <u>4</u> ears of sweet corn in each bag.

Singapore Math Practice Level 2A

Look at the pictures carefully, and fill in each blank with the correct answer.

1.

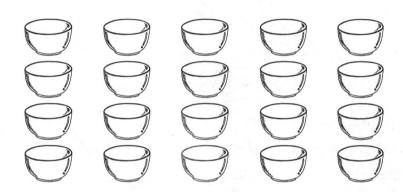

6 twos = _____

6 × 2 = _____

2.

5 fours = _____

5 × 4 = _____

3.

7 threes = _____

7 × 3 = _____

Singapore Math Practice Level 2A

4.

5 fives = _____

5 × 5 = _____

5.

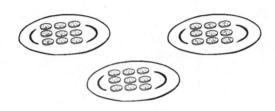

3 nines = _____

3 × 9 = _____

Study the pictures below. Fill in each blank with the correct answer.

6.

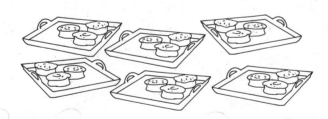

____ + ____ + ____ + ____ + ____ + ____ = _____

7.

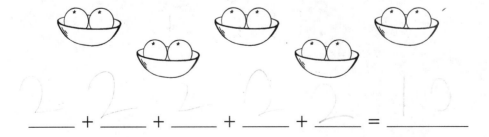

____ + ____ + ____ + ____ + ____ = _____

32

8.

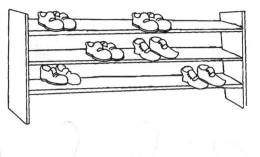

_____ + _____ + _____ = _____

9.

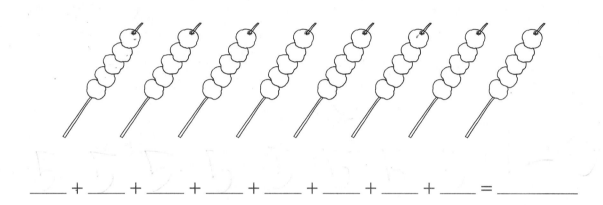

_____ + _____ + _____ + _____ + _____ + _____ + _____ + _____ = _____

10.

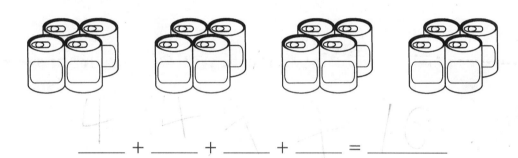

_____ + _____ + _____ + _____ = _____

Look at the pictures carefully, and fill in each blank with the correct answer.

11.

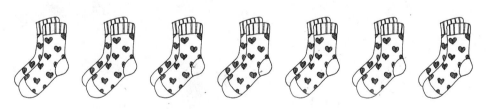

7 × _____ = _____

Singapore Math Practice Level 2A

12.

_____ × 5 = _____

13.

2 × _____ = _____

14.

5 × _____ = _____

15.

_____ × 4 = _____

Singapore Math Practice Level 2A

16. There are 3 kittens on each mat.

_____ × _____ = _____

There are _____ kittens altogether.

17. There are 10 eggs on each tray.

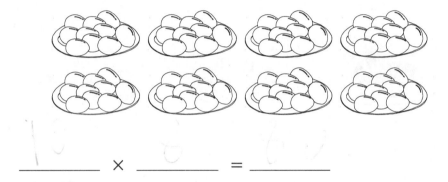

_____ × _____ = _____

There are _____ eggs altogether.

18. There are 4 teddy bears in each group.

_____ × _____ = _____

There are _____ teddy bears altogether.

Singapore Math Practice Level 2A

19. There are 5 magazines on each shelf.

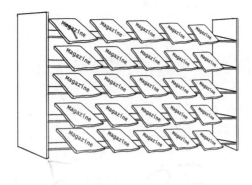

_____ × _____ = _____

There are _____ magazines altogether.

20. There are 7 pieces of candy in each box.

_____ × _____ = _____

There are _____ pieces of candy altogether.

21. Divide 12 balls into 3 equal groups.

12 ÷ _____ = _____

There are _____ balls in each group.

Singapore Math Practice Level 2A

22. Divide 20 bottle caps into 2 equal groups.

$$20 \div \text{_____} = \text{_____}$$

There are _____ bottle caps in each group.

23. Divide 9 hats into groups of 3.

$$9 \div \text{_____} = \text{_____}$$

There are _____ groups of hats.

24. Divide 20 ice-cream cones into groups of 4.

$$20 \div \text{_____} = \text{_____}$$

There are _____ groups of ice-cream cones.

Singapore Math Practice Level 2A

25. Divide 18 pens into groups of 3.

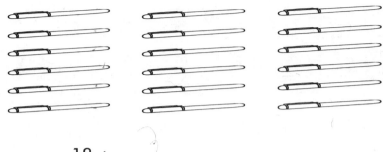

$18 \div$ _____ $=$ _____

There are _____ groups of pens.

Write 2 multiplication and division sentences for each set of pictures.

26.

_____ $\times$ _____ $=$ _____   _____ $\times$ _____ $=$ _____

_____ $\div$ _____ $=$ _____   _____ $\div$ _____ $=$ _____

27.

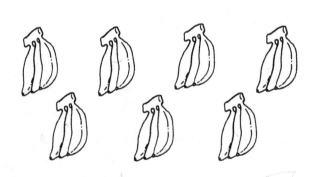

_____ $\times$ _____ $=$ _____   _____ $\times$ _____ $=$ _____

_____ $\div$ _____ $=$ _____   _____ $\div$ _____ $=$ _____

Singapore Math Practice Level 2A

28.

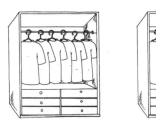  

_____ × _____ = _____   _____ × _____ = _____

_____ ÷ _____ = _____   _____ ÷ _____ = _____

29.

_____ × _____ = _____   _____ × _____ = _____

_____ ÷ _____ = _____   _____ ÷ _____ = _____

30.

_____ × _____ = _____   _____ × _____ = _____

_____ ÷ _____ = _____   _____ ÷ _____ = _____

REVIEW 2

Look at the pictures carefully, and fill in each blank with the correct answer.

1.

7 twos = _____

7 × 2 = _____

2.

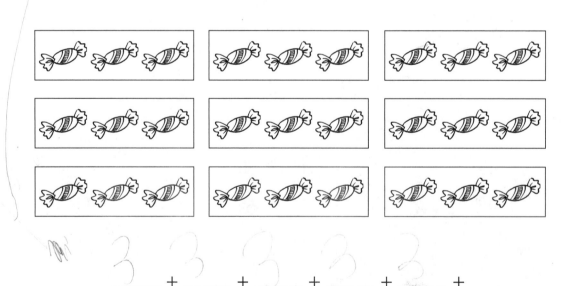

____ + ____ + ____ + ____ + ____ +

____ + ____ + ____ + ____ = _____

Singapore Math Practice Level 2A

Write 2 multiplication and division sentences for each set of pictures.

3.

_____ × _____ = _____   _____ × _____ = _____

_____ ÷ _____ = _____   _____ ÷ _____ = _____

4.

_____ × _____ = _____   _____ × _____ = _____

_____ ÷ _____ = _____   _____ ÷ _____ = _____

Study the pictures carefully, and fill in each blank with the correct answer.

5.   Divide 15 spoons into 3 equal groups.

15 ÷ _____ = _____

There are _____ spoons in each group.

Singapore Math Practice Level 2A

6. Divide 32 pieces of candy into groups of 4.

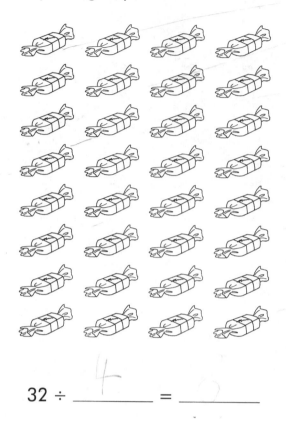

$$32 \div \underline{\hspace{2cm}} = \underline{\hspace{2cm}}$$

There are _____ groups of candy.

7. Divide 14 socks into 2 equal groups.

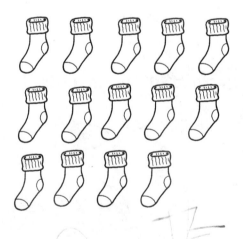

$$14 \div \underline{\hspace{2cm}} = \underline{\hspace{2cm}}$$

There are _____ socks in each group.

Singapore Math Practice Level 2A

8. There are 6 flowers in each vase.

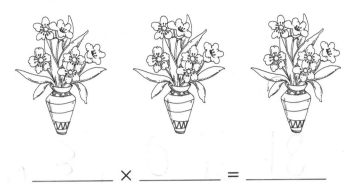

_____ × _____ = _____

There are _____ flowers altogether.

9. There are 5 buttons on each shirt.

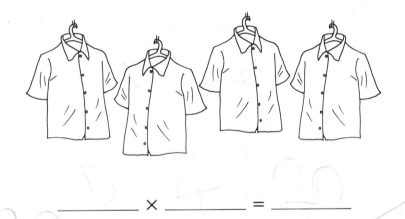

_____ × _____ = _____

There are _____ buttons altogether.

10. There are 3 lollipops in each bowl.

_____ × _____ = _____

There are _____ lollipops altogether.

Singapore Math Practice Level 2A

Draw the models, and solve the following story problems.

11. Abby has 796 stickers in her collection. Her sister gives her another 159 stickers. How many stickers does Abby have?

Abby has _____ stickers.

12. Jaya has 187 oranges. She uses 93 oranges to make some juice for a party. How many oranges does she have left?

She has _____ oranges left.

13. Benjamin scored 96 on his English test. He scored 82 on his math test. What was his combined score for both tests?

He scored _____ on both tests combined.

Singapore Math Practice Level 2A

14. (a) Mrs. Anderson baked 455 cookies at her bakery on Saturday. She baked 380 cookies on Sunday. How many cookies did she bake during the weekend?

She baked _____ cookies during the weekend.

(b) She gave 172 cookies to her son's school. How many cookies did she have left?

She had _____ cookies left.

15. Katrina has 496 books. Isabel has 388 books. How many books do they have in all?

They have _____ books in all.

16. Cameron spent $285 on a trip to Florida. Antonio spent $62 less than Cameron. How much did Antonio spend?

Antonio spent $_____.

17. Dmitri has 9 marbles. Adrian has 8 marbles. Zackary has 6 marbles. How many marbles do the 3 boys have altogether?

    The 3 boys have _____ marbles altogether.

18. Mr Simon had 245 oranges and 379 apples. 188 pieces of fruit were rotten. How many pieces of fruit did Mr. Simon have left?

    Mr. Simon had _____ pieces of fruit left.

19. Kaylee spent $503 in June. She spent $128 less in June than in July. How much did she spend in July?

    She spent $_____ in July.

20. 586 visitors went to the zoo in November. 253 fewer vistors went to the zoo in December. How many visitors went to the zoo in these 2 months?

    _____ visitors went to the zoo in these 2 months.

Singapore Math Practice Level 2A

Unit 5: MULTIPLYING AND DIVIDING NUMBERS BY 2 AND 3

Examples:

1. Rick has 3 notebooks.

   There are 10 pages in each notebook.

   How many pages are there in all?

   $$3 \times 10 = 30$$

   There are **30** pages in all.

2. Mrs. Mendoza has 18 carrots.

   She gives each rabbit 2 carrots.

   How many rabbits does she give all her carrots to?

   $$18 \div 2 = 9$$

   She gives all her carrots to **9** rabbits.

1. Fill in each blank by counting in twos.

2. Fill in each blank by counting in threes.

Singapore Math Practice Level 2A

Fill in each blank with the correct answer.

3. $4 \times 2 =$ _____

4. $6 \times 2 =$ _____

5. $5 \times 3 =$ _____

6. $8 \times 2 =$ _____

7. $9 \times 3 =$ _____

8. $3 \times 3 =$ _____

9. $7 \times 3 =$ _____

10. $9 \times 2 =$ _____

11. $6 \times 3 =$ _____

12. $5 \times 2 =$ _____

Fill in each blank with the correct answer.

13. _____ $\times 2 = 20$

14. _____ $\times 3 = 15$

15. $2 \times$ _____ $= 12$

16. $3 \times$ _____ $= 9$

17. $3 \times$ _____ $= 18$

18. $3 \times$ _____ $= 27$

19. $2 \times$ _____ $= 10$

20. _____ $\times 3 = 12$

21. _____ $\times 2 = 16$

22. _____ $\times 2 = 18$

Fill in each blank with the correct answer.

23. $30 \div 3 =$ _____

24. $21 \div 3 =$ _____

25. $16 \div 2 =$ _____

26. $18 \div 3 =$ _____

27. $14 \div 2 =$ _____

28. $8 \div 2 =$ _____

29. $12 \div 2 =$ _____

30. $15 \div 3 =$ _____

31. $10 \div 2 =$ _____

32. $24 \div 3 =$ _____

Singapore Math Practice Level 2A

33. Match each car to the correct owner.

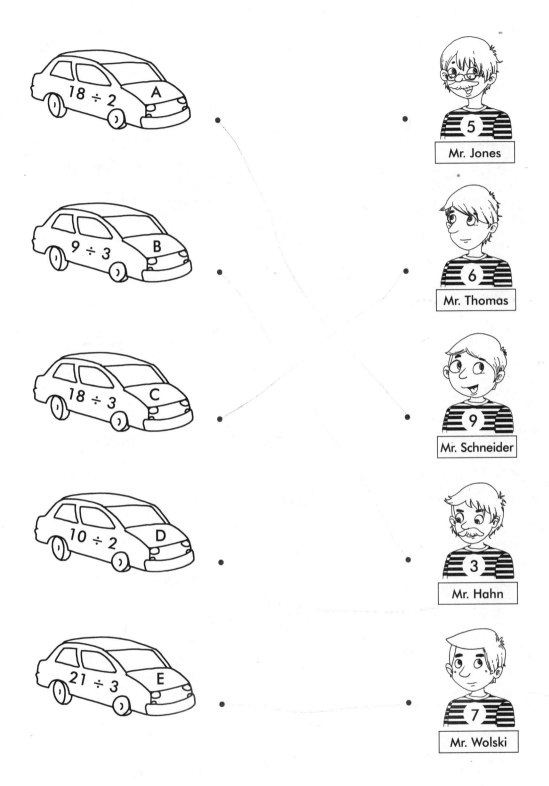

Singapore Math Practice Level 2A

Solve the following story problems. Show your work in the space below.

34. Taylor bought 4 boxes of cake. There were 3 pieces of cake in each box. How many pieces of cake were there altogether?

There were _____ pieces of cake altogether.

35. There are 3 stars on a flag. There are 7 flags. How many stars are there altogether?

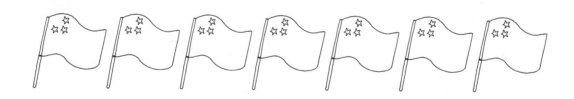

There are _____ stars altogether.

Singapore Math Practice Level 2A

36. Each tricycle has 3 wheels. There are 15 wheels altogether. How many tricycles are there?

There are _____ tricycles.

37. Eliza baked 14 muffins. She gave 2 muffins to each of her friends. How many friends did she give the muffins to?

She gave the muffins to _____ friends.

38. Minh packs 3 tennis balls into each bag. If there are 27 tennis balls, how many bags will she need?

She will need _____ bags.

Singapore Math Practice Level 2A

39. The picture below shows several items sold at a drugstore.

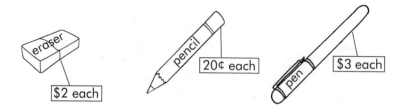

(a) Jane buys 4 erasers. How much does she pay in all?

$_____

(b) Luke has $12. How many pens can he buy?

_____ pens

(c) Ken buys 3 pens. How much does he pay altogether?

$_____

(d) Jade has $16. How many erasers can she buy?

_____ erasers

(e) There are 4 students in a group. If Mrs. Moran gives 3 pencils to each student, how many pencils does she need to buy?

_____ pencils

40. Complete the crossword puzzle with the correct answers.

12	÷		=	6
÷				×
	÷		=	
=				=
	×	9	=	18

Singapore Math Practice Level 2A

Unit 6: MULTIPLYING AND DIVIDING NUMBERS BY 4, 5, AND 10

Examples:

1. There are 10 SUVs in a parking lot.

    Each SUV has 4 wheels.

    How many wheels are there altogether?

    $$10 \times 4 = 40$$

    There are **40** wheels altogether.

2. Uncle Ron works 5 days each week.

    How many days does he work in 8 weeks?

    $$8 \times 5 = 40$$

    He works **40** days in 8 weeks.

3. There are 80 pens.

    Andre ties 10 pens in each bundle.

    How many bundles of pens does Andre tie?

    $$80 \div 10 = 8$$

    Andre ties **8** bundles of pens.

Singapore Math Practice Level 2A

Complete the following tables.

1. Each car has 4 wheels.

Number of cars	1	2	4	7	9
Number of wheels	4	8	16	28	36

2. Each hand has 5 fingers.

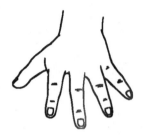

Number of hands	2	4	6	9	10
Number of fingers	10	20	30	45	50

3. Each vase has 10 flowers.

Number of vases	3	5	7	8	10
Number of flowers	30	50	70		100

Singapore Math Practice Level 2A

Fill in each blank with the correct answer.

4. $6 \times 4 =$ _____

5. $3 \times 5 =$ _____

6. $6 \times 5 =$ _____

7. $9 \times 5 =$ _____

8. $3 \times 10 =$ _____

9. $8 \times 10 =$ _____

10. $9 \times 4 =$ _____

11. $7 \times 10 =$ _____

12. $2 \times 4 =$ _____

13. $7 \times 5 =$ _____

Fill in each blank with the correct answer.

14. $30 \div 5 =$ _____

15. $20 \div 10 =$ _____

16. $16 \div 4 =$ _____

17. $40 \div 5 =$ _____

18. $24 \div 4 =$ _____

19. $90 \div 10 =$ _____

20. $12 \div 4 =$ _____

21. $100 \div 10 =$ _____

22. $10 \div 5 =$ _____

23. $40 \div 10 =$ _____

Write 2 multiplication and division sentences for each set of pictures.

24.

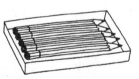

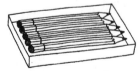
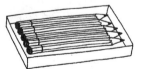

_____ × _____ = _____   _____ ÷ _____ = _____

_____ × _____ = _____   _____ ÷ _____ = _____

Singapore Math Practice Level 2A

25.

_____ × _____ = _____   _____ ÷ _____ = _____

_____ × _____ = _____   24 ÷ _____ = _____

26.

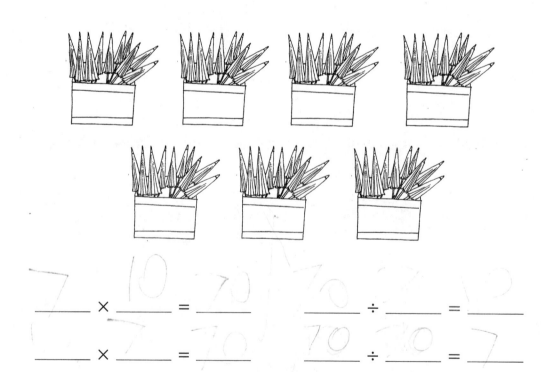

_____ × _____ = _____   _____ ÷ _____ = _____

_____ × _____ = _____   _____ ÷ _____ = _____

Singapore Math Practice Level 2A

27.

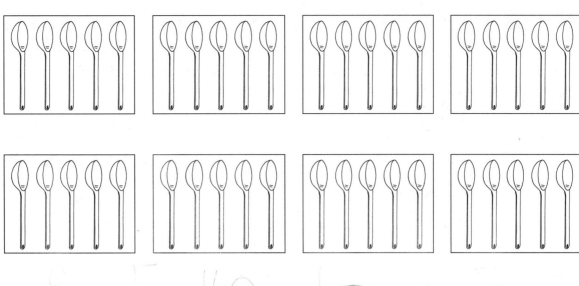

$\underline{8} \times \underline{5} = \underline{40}$

$\underline{} \div \underline{50} = \underline{}$

$\underline{5} \times \underline{} = \underline{}$

$\underline{50} \div \underline{50} = \underline{}$

28.

$\underline{3} \times \underline{4} = \underline{12}$

$\underline{12} \div \underline{3} = \underline{12}$

$\underline{12} \times \underline{12} = \underline{12}$

$\underline{12} \div \underline{12} = \underline{}$

Singapore Math Practice Level 2A

Solve the following story problems. Show your work in the space below.

29. Mom buys 6 bags of apples. There are 5 apples in each bag. How many apples are there altogether?

    There are _____ apples altogether.

30. Sam spends $10 every week. How much does he spend in 8 weeks?

    Sam spends $_____ in 8 weeks.

31. Leyla bought 4 meters of fabric. Each meter cost $7. How much did Leyla spend altogether?

    Leyla spent $_____ altogether.

Singapore Math Practice Level 2A

32. Dad sews 15 buttons on 3 shirts. How many buttons are there on each shirt?

There are _____ buttons on each shirt.

33. Alicia packs 10 packages of crackers into each bag. If there are 100 packages of crackers, how many bags does Alicia need?

Alicia needs _____ bags.

34. Maggy saves $5 every month. How much will she save in 10 months?

Maggy will save $_____ in 10 months.

Unit 7: FUN WITH MODELS (MULTIPLYING AND DIVIDING)

Examples:

1. Gigi uses 5 oranges to make a glass of juice.

    She makes 7 glasses of juice.

    How many oranges does she use altogether?

    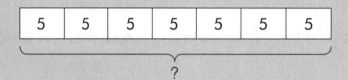

    $7 \times 5 = 35$

    She uses **35** oranges altogether.

2. Yumi spent $24 on some T-shirts.

    Each T-shirt cost $6.

    How many T-shirts did she buy?

    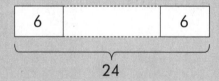

    $\$24 \div \$6 = 4$

    She bought **4** T-shirts.

Singapore Math Practice Level 2A

Draw the models, and solve the following story problems.

1. There are 5 albums. Each album contains 10 stamps. How many stamps are there in all?

    There are _____ stamps in all.

2. There are 3 eggs in a bag. How many eggs are there in 6 bags?

    There are _____ eggs in 6 bags.

3. Grace and 4 friends share 30 oranges equally. How many oranges does each of them have?

    Each of them has _____ oranges.

Singapore Math Practice Level 2A

4. Hakeem buys 4 packets of stickers. There are 9 stickers in each packet. How many stickers does he buy?

He buys _____ stickers.

5. Kelly bought 18 sunflowers. She placed on equal number into 2 vases. How many sunflowers were there in each vase?

There were _____ sunflowers in each vase.

6. Ms. Drew gave 36 markers to some children. Each child received 4 markers. How many children did Ms. Drew give the markers to?

Ms. Drew gave the markers to _____ children.

Singapore Math Practice Level 2A

7. Each child has 7 library books. How many books do 5 children have?

    5 children have _____ library books.

8. Mom bought 21 rolls. She placed 3 rolls on each plate. How many plates did she use?

    She used _____ plates.

Singapore Math Practice Level 2A

REVIEW 3

Match each kite to the correct girl.

1.

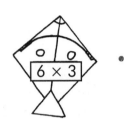

24

2.

15

3.

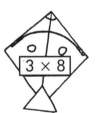

18

4.

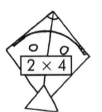

8

5.

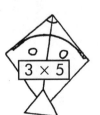

14

64

Fill in each blank with the correct answer.

6. $80 \div 10 =$ _____

7. $45 \div 5 =$ _____

8. $12 \div 2 =$ _____

9. $24 \div 3 =$ _____

10. $28 \div 4 =$ _____

11. _____ $\times 4 = 16$

12. $10 \times$ _____ $= 20$

13. $6 \times$ _____ $= 18$

14. _____ $\times 5 = 25$

15. _____ $\times 10 = 100$

Draw the models, and solve the following story problems.

16. There are 6 pencils in a box. How many pencils are there in 4 boxes?

There are _____ pencils in 4 boxes.

17. Zoe and 3 cousins shared a sum of $36. How much did each of them receive?

Each of them received $_____.

Singapore Math Practice Level 2A

18. Dad makes 50 muffins. He gives all the muffins to some friends. Each friend receives 5 muffins. How many friends does Dad give the muffins to?

Dad gives the muffins to _____ friends.

19. There are 30 pieces of colored paper in a package. There are 6 different colors. How many pieces of each color are there if the package contains an equal number of pieces for each color?

There are _____ pieces of each color.

20. Mrs. Yamamoto has 4 children. She buys a pair of gloves for each child. How many gloves does she buy?

She buys _____ gloves.

66

Unit 8: LENGTH

Examples:

1.

   What is the length of the card shown above?

   $$12 - 3 = 9$$

   The length of the card is **9 cm**.

2. Charlotte walked 345 yd. to a café.
   She walked another 150 yd. to the park.
   How far did she walk in all?

345 yd.	150 yd.

   ?

   $$345 + 150 = 495$$

   She walked **495 yd.** in all.

3. Fanny sews 4 pieces of ribbon to each side of a square cushion.
   If she uses 36 cm of ribbon altogether, what is the length of each piece of ribbon?

?	?	?	?

   36 cm

   $$36 \div 4 = 9$$

   The length of each piece of ribbon is **9 cm**.

Singapore Math Practice Level 2A

Write _more_ or _less_ on the lines.

1. The height of a flagpole is _____ than 1 m.

2. The length of a box of tissues is _____ than 1 m.

3. The length of a pencil is _____ than 1 m.

4. The height of a four-story school is _____ than 1 m.

5. The length of a workbook is _____ than 1 m.

Fill in each blank with the correct answer.

6. Ribbon A | 2 yd. |

     Ribbon B | 6 yd. |

     Ribbon C | 4 yd. |

(a) Ribbon _____ is the shortest.

(b) Ribbon _____ is the longest.

(c) Ribbon A is _____ yd. shorter than Ribbon C.

(d) Ribbon C is _____ yd. shorter than Ribbon B.

(e) Ribbon B is _____ yd. longer than Ribbon C.

(f) Ribbon B is _____ yd. longer than Ribbon A.

7.

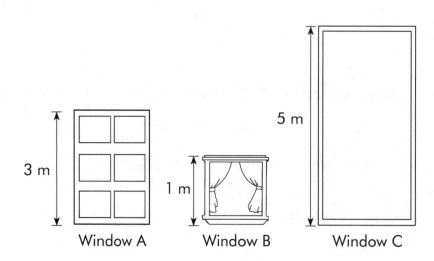

       3 m   1 m   5 m

        Window A   Window B   Window C

Singapore Math Practice Level 2A

(a) Window _____ is the tallest.

(b) Window _____ is the shortest.

(c) Window A is _____ m shorter than Window C.

(d) Window B is _____ m shorter than Window A.

(e) Window C is _____ m taller than Window B.

(f) Window C is _____ m taller than Window A.

8. Use a ruler to draw a line 4 in. long. Label it XY.

9. Use a ruler to draw a line 6 in. long. Label it WX.

10. Use a ruler to draw a line 5 in. long. Label it YZ.

Measure the following items with a ruler, and answer questions 11 to 14.

11.

The pen is _____ cm long.

12.

The envelope is _____ cm long.

13.

The notebook is _____ cm wide.

14.

The calculator is _____ cm wide.

Fill in each blank with *longer than* **or** *shorter than***.**

15. A _____   B _____

Line B is _____ Line A.

Singapore Math Practice Level 2A

16. A _____   B _____

Line A is _____ Line B.

17. A _____   B _____

Line A is _____ Line B.

18. Study the picture carefully. Fill in each blank with the correct answer.

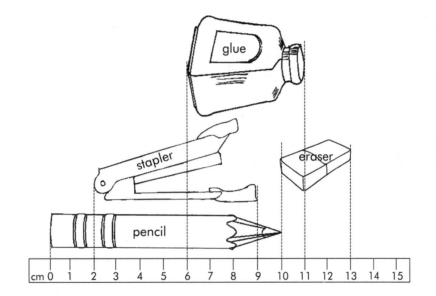

(a) The stapler is _____ cm long.

(b) The eraser is _____ cm long.

(c) The bottle of glue is _____ cm long.

(d) The pencil is _____ cm long.

(e) The eraser is _____ cm shorter than the pencil.

(f) The stapler is _____ cm longer than the bottle of glue.

(g) The longest item is the _____.

(h) The shortest item is the _____.

Singapore Math Practice Level 2A

19.

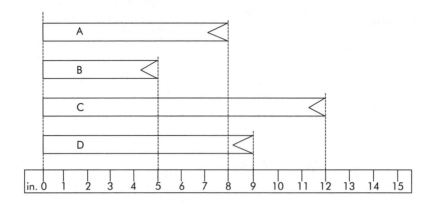

(a) Ribbon A is _____ in. long.

(b) Ribbon B is _____ in. long.

(c) Ribbon C is _____ in. long.

(d) Ribbon D is _____ in. long.

(e) Ribbon _____ is the longest.

(f) Ribbon _____ is the shortest.

(g) Ribbon C is _____ in. longer than Ribbon A.

(h) Ribbon D is 3 in. shorter than Ribbon _____.

Fill in each blank with the correct answer.

20. 38 in. + 78 in.　　　= _____ in.

21. 125 cm − 89 cm　　= _____ cm

22. 236 yd. + 279 yd.　= _____ yd.

23. 468 cm − 318 cm　= _____ cm

24. 200 yd. − 65 yd.　　= _____ yd.

25. 399 m + 121 m　　= _____ m

Singapore Math Practice Level 2A

Solve the following story problems. Show your work in the space below. Draw the appropriate models.

26. Miles sewed 278 in. of curtains on Monday. He sewed 516 in. of curtains on Tuesday. Find the total length of curtains Miles sewed on both days.

The total length of curtains Miles sewed on both days was _____ in.

27.

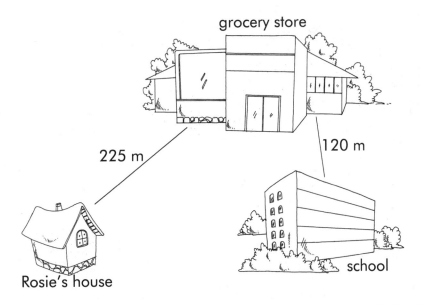

After school, Rosie goes to the grocery store to buy some milk before going home. How far does she travel?

She travels _____ m.

28. The stadium is 350 yd. away from Samir's house. Samir jogs to the stadium and back to his house. How far does he jog?

He jogs _____ yd.

29. Kate has a piece of ribbon 26 cm long. June has a piece of ribbon that is 13 cm shorter than Kate's ribbon.

(a) What is the length of June's ribbon?

June's ribbon is _____ cm long.

(b) Find the total length of the 2 ribbons.

The total length of the 2 ribbons is _____ cm long.

30. Nicholas placed 3 boxes side by side. The length of each box was 10 in. What was the length of the 3 boxes?

The length of the 3 boxes was _____ in.

31. Juan placed 8 toothpicks along a straight line. The length of each toothpick was 5 cm. What was the length of 8 toothpicks?

The length of 8 toothpicks was _____ cm.

32. Mr. Oliver cuts a rope that is 6 ft. long into 2 equal pieces. What is the length of each piece of rope?

The length of each piece of rope is _____ ft.

Singapore Math Practice Level 2A

33. Leo tears a strip of paper that is 27 cm long into equal pieces. Each piece of paper measures 3 cm. How many pieces of paper does Leo have?

Leo has _____ pieces of paper.

34. The length of a piece of string is 32 in. Gabrielle cuts the string into equal pieces. Each piece of string measures 4 in. How many pieces of string does Gabrielle have?

Gabrielle has _____ pieces of string.

Singapore Math Practice Level 2A

Unit 9: MASS

Examples:

1. What is the mass of the bag of sugar below?

    4 oz.

2. The mass of a bag of fruit is 12 kg. The mass of a bag of raisins is 7 kg lighter than the bag of fruit. What is the mass of the bag of raisins?

Fruit	12 kg
Raisins	?

    7 kg

    12 − 7 = 5

    The mass of the bag of raisins is **5 kg**.

3. Mrs. Giggs has 5 identical packages. Each package has a mass of 3 lb. What is the mass of all 5 packages?

3	3	3	3	3

    ?

    5 × 3 = 15

    The mass of all 5 packages is **15 lb**.

Singapore Math Practice Level 2A

Fill in each blank with *more than* **or** *less than.*

1.

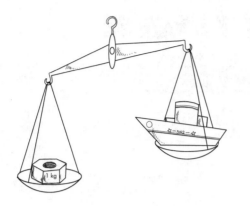

The mass of the toy ship is _____ 1 kg.

2.

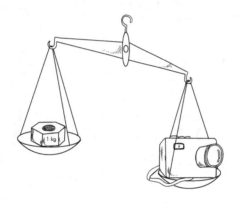

The mass of the camera is _____ 1 kg.

3.

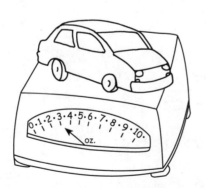

The mass of the toy car is _____ 4 oz.

Singapore Math Practice Level 2A

4.

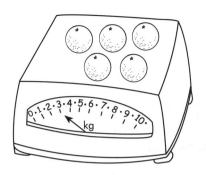

The mass of the oranges is _____ 2 kg.

5.

The mass of the boy is _____ 50 lb.

Look at each picture carefully. Write the correct mass on the lines provided.

6.

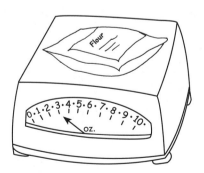

_____ oz.

Singapore Math Practice Level 2A

7.

_____ lb.

8.

_____ oz.

9.

_____ kg

10.

_____ kg

Singapore Math Practice Level 2A

11. Study the pictures below, and fill in each blank with the correct answer.

(a) The mass of the watermelon is _____ kg.

(b) The mass of the bunch of bananas is _____ kg.

(c) The mass of the pineapple is _____ kg.

(d) The _____ is the heaviest.

(e) The _____ is the lightest.

(f) Arrange the fruit in order. Begin with the heaviest fruit.

_____

Singapore Math Practice Level 2A

12. Study the pictures below, and fill in each blank with the correct answer.

Alan   Susan   Anne

(a)   Alan has a mass of _____ lb.

(b)   Susan has a mass of _____ lb.

(c)   Anne has a mass of _____ lb.

(d)   _____ is the lightest.

(e)   _____ is the heaviest.

(f)   Arrange them in order. Begin with the lightest mass.

_____

Singapore Math Practice Level 2A

Look at each picture carefully. Fill in each blank with the correct answer.

13.

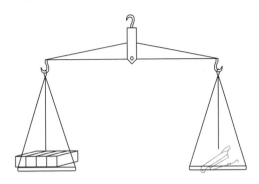

The mass of each ☐ is 1 g.

The stapler is _____ g.

14.

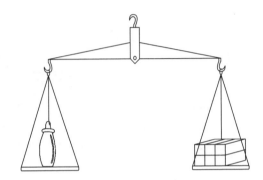

The mass of each ☐ is 1 oz.

The bottle is _____ oz.

15.

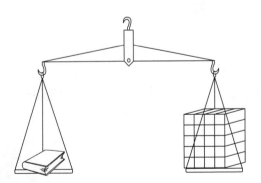

The mass of each ☐ is 1 g.

The dictionary is _____ g.

Singapore Math Practice Level 2A

16.

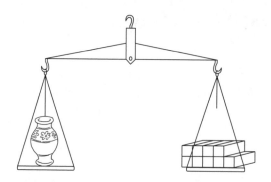

The mass of each ▭ is 1 oz.

The toy vase is _____ oz.

17.

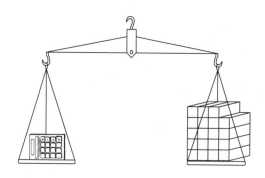

The mass of each ▭ is 1 g.

The calculator is _____ g.

Look at the following kitchen scales. Fill in each blank with the correct answer. Include the unit in your answer.

18.

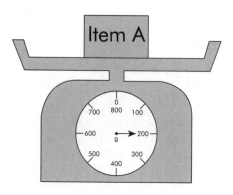

_____

19.

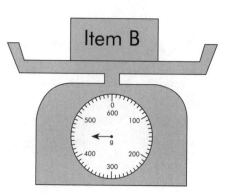

_____

Singapore Math Practice Level 2A

20.

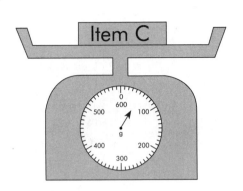

_____

21.

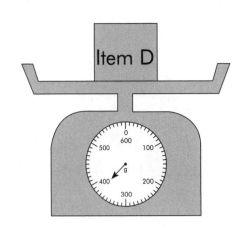

_____

Fill in each blank with the correct answer. Include the unit in your answer.

22.

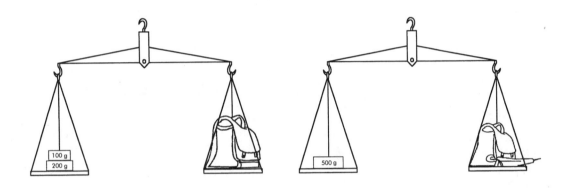

The umbrella has a mass of _____.

23.

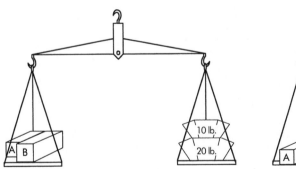 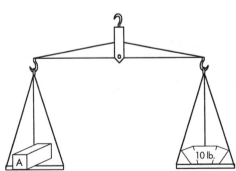

Box B has a mass of _____.

24.

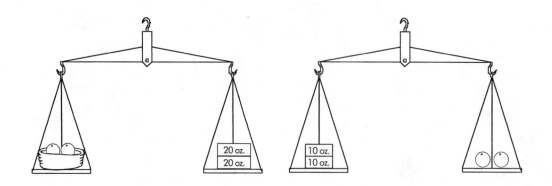

(a) The basket of oranges has a mass of _____.

(b) The oranges have a mass of _____.

(c) The basket has a mass of _____.

25.

(a) The teddy bear has a mass of _____.

(b) The teddy bear and the doll have a mass of _____.

(c) The doll has a mass of _____.

Singapore Math Practice Level 2A

26. Sam has a pet at home. Fill in each blank with the correct answer, and match the letters to the numbers in the boxes below. The first one has been done for you. Find out what pet Sam has at home.

(a) 14 kg + 15 kg = | 29 kg | M |

(b) 20 oz. + 15 oz. = | | R |

(c) 360 g + 250 g = | | A |

(d) 170 lb. + 360 lb. = | | S |

(e) 415 g + 235 g = | | E |

(f) 509 lb. + 137 lb. = | | T |

(g) 816 g + 45 g = | | H |

| | | M | | | | |
| 861 | 610 | 29 | 530 | 646 | 650 | 35 |

27. Adam's birthday is coming soon. Fill in each blank with the correct answer, and match the letters to the numbers to find out what Adam wants for his birthday.

(a)   585 oz. – 232 oz. = [| S]

(b)   616 kg – 307 kg = [| Z]

(c)   900 lb. – 450 lb. = [| U]

(d)   369 kg – 180 kg = [| L]

(e)   838 lb. – 639 lb. = [| E]

(f)   620 g – 505 g = [| P]

(g)   246 oz. – 97 oz. = [| Z]

[ ]   [ ]   [ ]   [ ]   [ ]   [ ]   [ ]

115   450   309   149   189   199   353

Singapore Math Practice Level 2A

Solve the following story problems. Show your work in the space below. Draw the appropriate models.

28. Aliyah uses 50 kg of flour, 14 kg of sugar, and 13 kg of butter to bake 10 cakes. How many kilograms of ingredients does she use altogether?

    She uses _____ kg of ingredients altogether.

29. Aidan has a mass of 43 lb. Tom is 10 lb. heavier than Aidan. What is Tom's mass?

    Tom's mass is _____ lb.

30. A contractor uses 83 kg of cement and sand to build a wall. If he uses 27 kg of sand, how much cement does he use?

    He uses _____ kg of cement.

Singapore Math Practice Level 2A

31. Angelo's family eats 13 oz. of rice every week. Noah's family eats 4 oz. less of rice. How much rice does Noah's family eat every week?

Noah's family eats _____ oz. of rice every week.

32. Kelly bought 380 g of meat. She then bought some fish. If the total mass of these 2 items was 945 g, how many grams of fish did she buy?

She bought _____ g of fish.

33. Aunt Rebecca bought 3 bags of tomatoes. Each bag had a mass of 2 lb. What was the total mass of the 3 bags of tomatoes?

The total mass of the 3 bags of tomatoes was _____ lb.

34. Colin bought 20 kg of flour. Each bag of flour had a mass of 5 kg. How many bags of flour did Colin buy?

Colin bought _____ bags of flour.

35. Priscilla has 10 plums. Each plum has a mass of 4 oz. What is the total mass of the 10 plums?

The total mass of the 10 plums is _____ oz.

36. Mom bought 12 kg of strawberries. She divided the strawberries equally into 4 bags. What was the mass of each bag?

The mass of each bag of strawberries was _____ kg.

Singapore Math Practice Level 2A

REVIEW 4

Fill in each blank with the correct answer.

1.

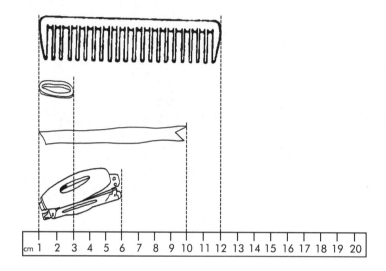

(a)   The hair clip is _____ cm long.

(b)   The ribbon is _____ cm long.

(c)   The comb is _____ cm long.

(d)   The rubber band is _____ cm long.

(e)   The ribbon is shorter than the comb by _____ cm.

(f)   The hair clip is longer than the rubber band by _____ cm.

(g)   The total length of the hair clip and the comb is _____ cm.

(h)   Arrange the items in order. Begin with the shortest.

_____

Singapore Math Practice Level 2A

2.

The mass of the watermelon is _____ oz.

3. Which line is the shortest?

A ————

B —————————

C —————————————

Line _____ is the shortest.

4.

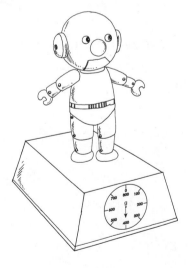

The mass of the toy robot is _____ g.

5.

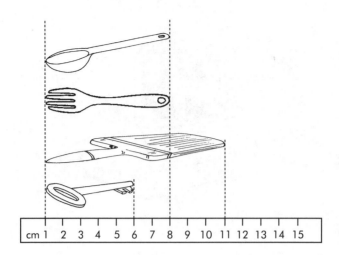

(a) The key is _____ cm long.

(b) The paintbrush is _____ cm long.

(c) The spoon is _____ cm long.

(d) The fork is _____ cm long.

(e) The key is shorter than the fork by _____ cm.

(f) The paintbrush is longer than the spoon by _____ cm.

(g) The _____ and _____ have the same length.

(h) Arrange the items in order. Begin with the longest.

_____

6.

The mass of the cat is _____ lb.

Singapore Math Practice Level 2A

7.

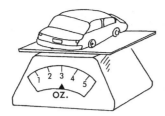 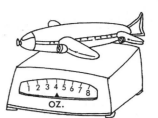

(a) The mass of the toy car is _____.

(b) The mass of the toy plane is _____.

(c) The mass of the toy ship is _____.

(d) The _____ is the heaviest.

(e) The _____ is the lightest.

8. Which line is the longest?

A ———

B ————

C —————

Line _____ is the longest.

Fill in each blank with *more than* or *less than*.

9.

The bag of rice is _____ 3 lb.

10.

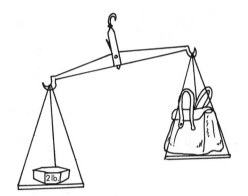

The purse is _____ 2 lb.

Fill in each blank with the correct answer.

11. 40 yd. + 68 yd. = _____ yd.

12. 435 in. − 79 in. = _____ in.

13. 616 in. − 327 in. = _____ in.

14. 125 ft. + 225 ft. = _____ ft.

15. 609 yd. + 163 yd. = _____ yd.

Singapore Math Practice Level 2A

Solve the following story problems. Show your work in the space below. Draw the appropriate models.

16.

360 m   525 m

supermarket   David's house   shopping center

How much farther is David's house from the shopping center than from the supermarket?

David's house is _____ m farther from the shopping center than from the supermarket.

17. Amanda jogs from her house to the stadium every day. Her jogging route is shown below.

375 yd.   425 yd.

Amanda's house   school   stadium

How far does Amanda jog from her house to the stadium?

Amanda jogs _____ yd. from her house to the stadium.

Singapore Math Practice Level 2A

18. Kenya came back from a trip. She brought along 2 pieces of luggage that weighed 8 lb. each. Find the total mass of her luggage.

The total mass of her luggage was _____ lb.

19. Jonathan bought some cherries. Each cherry had a mass of 3 g. The total mass of the cherries was 15 g. How many cherries did he buy?

He bought _____ cherries.

20. Su-Lin placed 5 rulers side by side. Each ruler had a length of 10 cm. What was the length of the 5 rulers?

The length of the 5 rulers was _____ cm.

Singapore Math Practice Level 2A

FINAL REVIEW

Fill in each blank with the correct answer.

1.

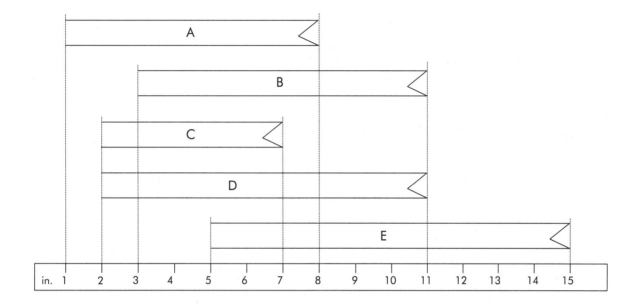

(a) Ribbon B is _____ in. long.

(b) Ribbon C is _____ in. long.

(c) Ribbon D is _____ in. long.

(d) Ribbon E is _____ in. long.

(e) The total length of ribbons A and C is _____ in.

(f) Arrange the ribbons in order. Begin with the longest.

_____

2.

The mass of the rabbit is _____ kg.

3. Write the number in words on the line.

   647 _____

4. Arrange the following numbers in order. Begin with the smallest.

415	303	540	405	330

   _____, _____, _____, _____, _____

5. The product of 3 and 9 is _____.

6. The sum of 237 and 508 is _____.

7. The difference between 717 and 169 is _____.

8. 10 more than 590 is _____.

9. 120 is 10 less than _____.

Singapore Math Practice Level 2A

10. Write 2 multiplication and division sentences using the pictures below.

_____ × _____ = _____   _____ × _____ = _____

_____ ÷ _____ = _____   _____ ÷ _____ = _____

11. Complete the number pattern.

660, _____, 700, 720, _____

12. Divide 24 bees into 4 equal groups.

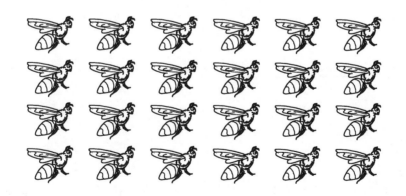

24 ÷ _____ = _____

There are _____ bees in each group.

Singapore Math Practice Level 2A

Fill in each blank with the correct answer.

13. (a)   105 cm + 68 cm = _____

    (b)   32 lb. − 16 lb. = _____

    (c)   _____ × 3 = 24

    (d)   612 + 258 = _____

    (e)   300 − 125 = _____

Write the correct answers on the lines.

14.   The table below shows the different colors of roses sold by a florist in a week.

red	315
yellow	197
white	280

    (a)   How many fewer yellow roses were sold than white ones?

    _____

    (b)   How many red and white roses were sold altogether?

    _____

15.   Omar wants to buy a remote-controlled airplane. It costs $65, but he has only $49. How much more money does he need?

    _____

16. Emily used 185 cm of cloth to sew some cushion covers. She used 275 cm of cloth to sew blankets. How much cloth did she use altogether?

_____

17. Michael has 35 baseball cards. He gives an equal number of cards to 5 friends. How many cards does each friend get?

_____

18. Mei baked 460 dog biscuits on Friday. She baked 150 fewer biscuits on Saturday.

    (a) How many dog biscuits did she bake on Saturday?

    _____

    (b) How many dog biscuits did she bake altogether?

    _____

19. Imani plants 3 rows of cacti in her garden. There are 7 cacti in each row. How many cacti does she plant altogether?

    _____

20. Vivian walks 150 yd. from her house to a store. She then walks another 180 yd. to a playground. How far does Vivian walk in all?

    _____

Singapore Math Practice Level 2A

Solve the following story problems. Show your work in the space below. Draw the appropriate models.

21. Dakota has 5 kiwi fruits. Each kiwi has a mass of 10 g. What is the total mass of the 5 kiwis?

22. Mrs. Coleman collected 32 pages of homework from a group of students. Each student turned in 4 pages. How many students did Mrs. Coleman collect the pages from?

Singapore Math Practice Level 2A

23. Hannah receives a daily allowance of $2. How much money does she receive from Monday to Friday?

24. 3 girls shared a piece of cloth equally. The total length of the piece of cloth was 9 yd. What was the length of cloth received by each girl?

25. A carpenter needs 4 days to build a bookshelf. How many days does he need to make 3 bookshelves?

CHALLENGE QUESTIONS

Solve the following problems on another sheet of paper.

1. Guess the 3-digit number based on the hints below.
    -   The first digit is greater than 7 and is an even number.
    -   The second digit is smaller than 7 and is the smallest odd number.
    -   The third digit is the difference between the first and the second digits.

2. Parker bought a skateboard for $126. He paid the cashier the exact amount with 10 bills. Identify the bills he used to pay for the skateboard.

3. Jessica has twice as many apples as Deepak. Deepak has 3 times as many apples as Gina. Gina has 2 apples. Draw a model, and find the number of apples Jessica has.

4. Mr. Schneider's mass is 2 digits. The first digit is 3 times the second digit. Both digits are odd numbers, and his mass is greater than 35 kg. What is Mr. Schneider's mass?

5. The sum of 2 facing pages of an opened dictionary can be divided by 3. The result of the division is 3. What are the 2 facing pages?

6. Carlos, Tyler, and Danny each have a ruler. Tyler's ruler is longer than Carlos's ruler but shorter than Danny's ruler. Who has the shortest ruler?

7. Jenna had a box of marbles. Her mother gave her twice the number of marbles Jenna already had. Her father gave her 3 times the number of marbles her mother gave her. Jenna had 27 marbles in the end. How many marbles did she have in the beginning?

Singapore Math Practice Level 2A

8. Simon had a bill. He used it to buy a shirt for $20 and received the change in four bills of the same amount. What was the bill that Simon had in the beginning?

9. The sum of 3 consecutive numbers, or 3 numbers in a row, is 9. What are the 3 numbers?

10. The sum of 2 facing pages of an opened comic book can be divided by 3. The result is 7. What are the 2 facing pages?

11. Mia is heavier than Dante but lighter than Sierra. Who is the heaviest among the 3 children?

Singapore Math Practice Level 2A

SOLUTIONS
Singapore Math Practice Level 2A

Unit 1: Numbers up to 1,000

1. 4 hundreds 2 tens 5 ones = **425**
2. 3 hundreds 8 tens 7 ones = **387**
3. 5 hundreds 3 tens = **530**
4. 8 hundreds 7 ones = **807**
5. 10 hundreds = **1,000**
6. **seven hundred and sixty**
7. **three hundred and seventy-eight**
8. **four hundred and fifty-six**
9. **two hundred and two**
10. **one thousand**
11. **562**
12. **779**
13. **110**
14. **358**
15. **907**
16. **8, 2, 5**
17. **6, 3, 0**
18. **7, 0, 5**
19. **4, 5, 9**
20. **10, 0, 0**
21. **tens**
22. **hundreds**
23. **hundreds**
24. **9**
25. **3**
26. **0**
27. **greater**
28. **smaller**
29. **smaller**
30. **greater**
31. **smaller**
32. **379, 397, 937, 973**
33. **129, 192, 219, 319**
34. **511, 571, 715, 751**
35. **116, 163, 313, 316**
36. **344, 404, 434, 443**
37. **750, 705, 570, 507**
38. **413, 341, 314, 134**
39. **960, 608, 517, 289, 187**
40. **857, 456, 320, 220, 190**
41. **970, 927, 727, 290, 279**
42. 10 + 560 = **570**
43. 680 − 20 = **660**
44. 100 + 778 = **878**
45. 695 − 200 = **495**
46. 279 − 5 = **274**
47. **300, 310**
    290 − 280 = 10
    290 + 10 = 300
    300 + 10 = 310
48. **670, 570**
    970 − 870 = 100
    770 − 100 = 670
    670 − 100 = 570
49. **780, 840**
    820 − 800 = 20
    760 + 20 = 780
    820 + 20 = 840
50. **490, 520**
    460 − 430 = 30
    460 + 30 = 490
    490 + 30 = 520
51. **450, 550**
    750 − 650 = 100
    650 − 100 = 550
    550 − 100 = 450

Unit 2: Adding and Subtracting Numbers 1-1,000

1.
```
    1 4 3
  + 2 1 4
  -------
    3 5 7
```

2.
```
    3 1 2
  + 4 8 1
  -------
    7 9 3
```

3.
```
    7 3 2
  + 1 4 5
  -------
    8 7 7
```

4.
```
    2 0 1
  + 2 8 3
  -------
    4 8 4
```

5.
```
    8 2 1
  + 1 6 3
  -------
    9 8 4
```

6.
```
    5 6 9
  − 2 3 4
  -------
    3 3 5
```

7.
```
    9 3 2
  − 1 2 1
  -------
    8 1 1
```

8.
```
    7 3 6
  − 2 0 4
  -------
    5 3 2
```

109

9.
```
   3 7 5
 - 1 5 2
   2 2 3
```

10.
```
   8 5 9
 - 6 0 7
   2 5 2
```

11.
```
   ¹
   1 3 5
 + 1 0 9
   2 4 4
```

12.
```
   ¹ ¹
   5 0 5
 + 2 9 5
   8 0 0
```

13.
```
   ¹
   7 3 7
 + 1 2 9
   8 6 6
```

14.
```
   ¹
   2 5 6
 + 3 8 0
   6 3 6
```

15.
```
   ¹
   4 6 2
 + 2 0 8
   6 7 0
```

16.
```
   ¹ ¹
   3 9 7
 + 5 4 6
   9 4 3
```

17.
```
   2 14 13
   3̶ 5̶ 3̶
 - 1 7 4
   1 7 9
```

18.
```
   6 11
   9 7̶ 1̶
 - 3 6 9
   6 0 2
```

19.
```
   3 9 10
   4̶ 0̶ 0̶
 - 2 0 5
   1 9 5
```

20.
```
   5 13
   6̶ 3̶ 2
 - 1 7 1
   4 6 1
```

21.
```
   3 10 12
   4̶ 1̶ 2̶
 - 1 2 4
   2 8 8
```

22.
```
   4 9 10
   5̶ 0̶ 0̶
 - 1 7 8
   3 2 2
```

23.
```
   7 10
   8̶ 0̶ 0
 - 2 8 0
   5 2 0
```

24.
```
   7 10
   9 8̶ 0̶
 - 5 5 5
   4 2 5
```

25.

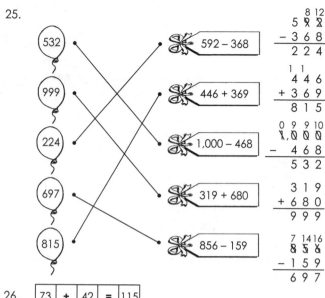

```
    8 12
    5 9̶ 2̶
  - 3 6 8
    2 2 4
```

```
    1 1
    4 4 6
  + 3 6 9
    8 1 5
```

```
    0 9 9 10
    1̶ 0̶ 0̶ 0̶
  -   4 6 8
      5 3 2
```

```
    3 1 9
  + 6 8 0
    9 9 9
```

```
    7 14 16
    8̶ 5̶ 6̶
  - 1 5 9
    6 9 7
```

26.
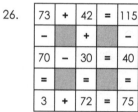

73	+	42	=	115
−		+		−
70	−	30	=	40
=		=		=
3	+	72	=	75

27.
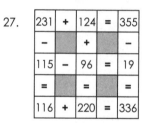

231	+	124	=	355
−		+		−
115	−	96	=	19
=		=		=
116	+	220	=	336

28.

Anne [?]
Lena [389] [317]

389 + 317 = 706

Anne collects **706** stickers.

```
    1 1
    3 8 9
  + 3 1 7
    7 0 6
```

29.

Tom [416]
John [?] [29]

416 − 29 = 387

John has **387** bottle caps.

```
    3 10 16
    4̶ 1̶ 6̶
  -     2 9
      3 8 7
```

30.

Monday	Tuesday
586	237
{ ? }

586 + 237 = 823

He sold **823** roses altogether.

```
    1 1
    5 8 6
  + 2 3 7
    8 2 3
```

31.

Saturday	Sunday
416	555
{ ? }

416 + 555 = 971

971 visitors were at the museum on both days.

```
      1
    4 1 6
  + 5 5 5
    9 7 1
```

110

32.

Marcus	Jack
?	$469

$837

```
  7 12 17
  8  3  7
-    4 6 9
     3 6 8
```

$837 − $469 = $368
Marcus spent **$368**.

Review 1

1. **three hundred and seventy-five**
2. **nine hundred and nineteen**
3. **212**
4. **303**
5. **917, 420, 402, 313, 179**
6. **128, 182, 218, 281, 812**
7. 10 + 360 = **370**
8. 876 − 50 = **826**
9. **516, 456**
   496 − 476 = 20
   536 − 20 = 516
   476 − 20 = 456

10.
```
    1
    6 0 8
  + 1 2 9
    7 3 7
```

11.
```
    1 1
    5 7 6
  + 1 8 8
    7 6 4
```

12.
```
    1
    1 5 4
  + 3 6 5
    5 1 9
```

13.
```
    1 1
    3 1 2
  + 4 9 8
    8 1 0
```

14.
```
    6 9 10
    7 0 0
  − 4 3 5
    2 6 5
```

15.
```
      1 18
    3 2 8
  − 1 0 9
    2 1 9
```

16.
```
    7 15 10
    8 6 0
  − 3 8 9
    4 7 1
```

17.
```
    4 13 12
    5 4 2
  − 3 7 9
    1 6 3
```

18. (a) 575 − 379 = 196

Wednesday	575
Monday	379 ?

```
    4 16 15
    5 7 5
  − 3 7 9
    1 9 6
```

196 more people went to the zoo on Wednesday than on Monday.

(b) 686 − 379 = 307

Tuesday	686
Monday	379 ?

```
      7 16
    6 8 6
  − 3 7 9
    3 0 7
```

---

307 fewer people went to the zoo on Monday than on Tuesday.

19.

1,000	
494	?

```
    0 9 9 10
    1 0 0 0
  −   4 9 4
      5 0 6
```

1,000 − 494 = 506
Aaron needs to collect **506** more stamps.

20.

?	
360	265

```
      1
    3 6 0
  + 2 6 5
    6 2 5
```

360 + 265 = 625
Jazmin sold **625** flowers on both days.

Unit 3: Fun with Models (Adding and Subtracting)

1.

576	186
?	

```
    1 1
    5 7 6
  + 1 8 6
    7 6 2
```

576 + 186 = 762
They have **762** bookmarks altogether.

2.

280	
168	?

```
      7 10
    2 8 0
  − 1 6 8
    1 1 2
```

280 − 168 = 112
He has **112** chickens left.

3.

?		
360	275	150

```
    1              
    3 6 0      6 3 5
  + 2 7 5    + 1 5 0
    6 3 5      7 8 5
```

360 + 275 + 150 = 785
He sold **785** oranges altogether.

4.

96	
78	?

```
    8 16
    9 6
  − 7 8
    1 8
```

96 − 78 = 18
She gave **18** seashells to her best friend.

5.

?	
131	280

```
      1
    1 3 1
  + 2 8 0
    4 1 1
```

131 + 280 = 411
He had **411** stamps altogether.

6.

216	137	97
?		

```
      1            1 1
    2 1 6      3 5 3
  + 1 3 7    +   9 7
    3 5 3      4 5 0
```

216 + 137 + 97 = 450
There are **450** animals on the farm.

7.

720	
465	?

```
    6 11 10
    7 2 0
  − 4 6 5
    2 5 5
```

720 − 465 = 255
He gave **255** trading cards to his brother.

8. (a)

Hitomi	$310
Brother	$280

```
    3 1 0
  + 2 8 0
    5 9 0
```

$310 + $280 = $590
Her brother saves **$590**.

(b)

$310	$590

$$\begin{array}{r} 1 \\ 3\ 1\ 0 \\ +\ 5\ 9\ 0 \\ \hline 9\ 0\ 0 \end{array}$$

$310 + $590 = $900
They save **$900** altogether.

Unit 4: Multiplying and Dividing

1. **12, 12**
   $2 + 2 + 2 + 2 + 2 + 2 = 12$
2. **20, 20**
   $4 + 4 + 4 + 4 + 4 = 20$
3. **21, 21**
   $3 + 3 + 3 + 3 + 3 + 3 + 3 = 21$
4. **25, 25**
   $5 + 5 + 5 + 5 + 5 = 25$
5. **27, 27**
   $9 + 9 + 9 = 27$
6. $3 + 3 + 3 + 3 + 3 + 3 = \mathbf{18}$
7. $2 + 2 + 2 + 2 + 2 = \mathbf{10}$
8. $4 + 4 + 4 = \mathbf{12}$
9. $5 + 5 + 5 + 5 + 5 + 5 + 5 + 5 = \mathbf{40}$
10. $4 + 4 + 4 + 4 = \mathbf{16}$
11. **2, 14**
12. **4, 20**
13. **8, 16**
14. **3, 15**
15. **4, 16**
16. **6, 3, 18, 18**
17. **8, 10, 80, 80**
18. **3, 4, 12, 12**
19. **5, 5, 25, 25**
20. **5, 7, 35, 35**
21. **3, 4, 4**

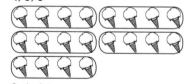

22. **2, 10, 10**

23. **3, 3, 3**

24. **4, 5, 5**

25. **3, 6, 6**

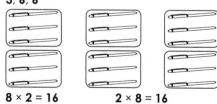

26. **8 × 2 = 16**   **2 × 8 = 16**
    16 ÷ 8 = 2   **16 ÷ 2 = 8**
27. **3 × 7 = 21**   **7 × 3 = 21**

28. 21 ÷ 3 = 7   21 ÷ 7 = 3
    3 × 6 = 18   6 × 3 = 18
    18 ÷ 3 = 6   18 ÷ 6 = 3
29. 6 × 4 = 24   4 × 6 = 24
    24 ÷ 6 = 4   24 ÷ 4 = 6
30. 4 × 3 = 12   3 × 4 = 12
    12 ÷ 4 = 3   12 ÷ 3 = 4

Review 2

1. **14, 14**
   $2 + 2 + 2 + 2 + 2 + 2 + 2 = 14$
2. $3 + 3 + 3 + 3 + 3 + 3 + 3 + 3 + 3 = \mathbf{27}$
3. **4 × 3 = 12**   **3 × 4 = 12**
   12 ÷ 4 = 3   **12 ÷ 3 = 4**
4. **5 × 2 = 10**   **2 × 5 = 10**
   10 ÷ 5 = 2   **10 ÷ 2 = 5**
5. **3, 5, 5**

6. **4, 8, 8**

7. **2, 7, 7**

8. **3 × 6 = 18, 18**
9. **4 × 5 = 20, 20**
10. **7 × 3 = 21, 21**
11.

796	159

?

$$\begin{array}{r} 1\ 1 \\ 7\ 9\ 6 \\ +\ 1\ 5\ 9 \\ \hline 9\ 5\ 5 \end{array}$$

796 + 159 = 955
Abby has **955** stickers.

12.

187

?	93

$$\begin{array}{r} 0\ 18 \\ \cancel{1}\ \cancel{8}\ 7 \\ -\ \ \ 9\ 3 \\ \hline 9\ 4 \end{array}$$

187 − 93 = 94
She has **94** oranges left.

13.

?

96	82

$$\begin{array}{r} 9\ 6 \\ +\ 8\ 2 \\ \hline 1\ 7\ 8 \end{array}$$

96 + 82 = 178
He scored **178** on both tests combined.

14. (a)

455	380

?

$$\begin{array}{r} 1 \\ 4\ 5\ 5 \\ +\ 3\ 8\ 0 \\ \hline 8\ 3\ 5 \end{array}$$

455 + 380 = 835
She baked **835** cookies during the weekend.

(b)

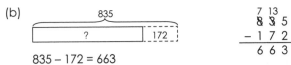

835 – 172 = 663
She had **663** cookies left.

$$
\begin{array}{r}
7\ \ 13 \\
8\ \cancel{3}\ 5 \\
-\ 1\ 7\ 2 \\
\hline
6\ 6\ 3
\end{array}
$$

15.

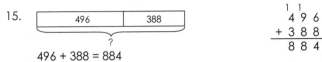

496 + 388 = 884
They have **884** books in all.

$$
\begin{array}{r}
1\ \ 1\ \ \\
4\ 9\ 6 \\
+\ 3\ 8\ 8 \\
\hline
8\ 8\ 4
\end{array}
$$

16.

| Cameron | $285 |
| Antonio | ? |

$62

$285 – $62 = $223
Antonio spent **$223**.

$$
\begin{array}{r}
2\ 8\ 5 \\
-\ \ \ 6\ 2 \\
\hline
2\ 2\ 3
\end{array}
$$

17.

| 9 | 8 | 6 |

?

9 + 8 + 6 = 23
The 3 boys have **23** marbles altogether.

18.

245 + 379

| ? | 188 |

245 + 379 = 624

624 – 188 = 436
Mr. Simon had **436** pieces of fruit left.

$$
\begin{array}{r}
1\ \ 1\ \ \\
2\ 4\ 5 \\
+\ 3\ 7\ 9 \\
\hline
6\ 2\ 4
\end{array}
\qquad
\begin{array}{r}
5\ \ 11\ 14 \\
\cancel{6}\ \cancel{2}\ \cancel{4} \\
-\ 1\ 8\ 8 \\
\hline
4\ 3\ 6
\end{array}
$$

19.

?

| July | | $128 |
| June | $503 | |

$503 + $128 = $631
She spent **$631** in July.

$$
\begin{array}{r}
1\ \ \\
5\ 0\ 3 \\
+\ 1\ 2\ 8 \\
\hline
6\ 3\ 1
\end{array}
$$

20.

| November | 586 |
| December | ? |

253

?

586 – 253 = 333

586 + 333 = 919

$$
\begin{array}{r}
5\ 8\ 6 \\
-\ 2\ 5\ 3 \\
\hline
3\ 3\ 3
\end{array}
\qquad
\begin{array}{r}
1\ \ \\
5\ 8\ 6 \\
+\ 3\ 3\ 3 \\
\hline
9\ 1\ 9
\end{array}
$$

919 visitors went to the zoo in these 2 months.

Unit 5: Multiplying and Dividing Numbers by 2 and 3

1. **6, 8, 12**
2. **9, 12, 18**
3. **8**
4. **12**
5. **15**
6. **16**
7. **27**
8. **9**
9. **21**
10. **18**
11. **18**
12. **10**
13. **10**
14. **5**
15. **6**
16. **3**

17. **6**
18. **9**
19. **5**
20. **4**
21. **8**
22. **9**
23. **10**
24. **7**
25. **8**
26. **6**
27. **7**
28. **4**
29. **6**
30. **5**
31. **5**
32. **8**
33.

34.

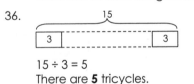

| 3 | 3 | 3 | 3 |

$4 \times 3 = 12$
There were **12** pieces of cakes altogether.

35.

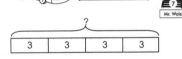

| 3 | 3 | 3 | 3 | 3 | 3 | 3 |

$7 \times 3 = 21$
There are **21** stars altogether.

36.

15

| 3 | | 3 |

$15 \div 3 = 5$
There are **5** tricycles.

37.

14

| 2 | | 2 |

$14 \div 2 = 7$
She gave the muffins to **7** friends.

38.

27

| 3 | | 3 |

$27 \div 3 = 9$
She will need **9** bags.

Singapore Math Practice Level 2A

39. (a) **8**

$4 \times \$2 = \$8$

(b) **4**

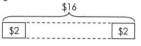

$\$12 \div \$3 = 4$

(c) **9**

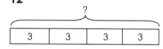

$3 \times \$3 = \$9$

(d) **8**

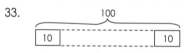

$\$16 \div \$2 = 8$

(e) **12**

$4 \times 3 = 12$

40.

12	÷	**2**	=	6
÷				×
6	÷	**2**	=	**3**
=				=
2	×	9	=	18

Unit 6: Multiplying and Dividing Numbers by 4, 5, and 10

1.
Number of cars	1	2	4	**7**	9
Number of wheels	4	8	**16**	28	**36**

$4 \times 4 = 16 \qquad 28 \div 4 = 7 \qquad 9 \times 4 = 36$

2.
Number of hands	2	**4**	6	**9**	10
Number of fingers	10	20	**30**	45	**50**

$20 \div 5 = 4 \qquad 6 \times 5 = 30 \qquad 45 \div 5 = 9 \qquad 10 \times 5 = 50$

3.
Number of vases	3	**5**	7	8	**10**
Number of flowers	30	50	**70**	**80**	100

$50 \div 10 = 5 \qquad 7 \times 10 = 70 \qquad 8 \times 10 = 80 \qquad 100 \div 10 = 10$

4. **24**
5. **15**
6. **30**
7. **45**
8. **30**
9. **80**
10. **36**
11. **70**
12. **8**

13. **35**
14. **6**
15. **2**
16. **4**
17. **8**
18. **6**
19. **9**
20. **3**
21. **10**
22. **2**
23. **4**
24. $5 \times 4 = 20$ $20 \div 5 = 4$
    $4 \times 5 = 20$ $20 \div 4 = 5$
25. $6 \times 4 = 24$ $24 \div 6 = 4$
    $4 \times 6 = 24$ $24 \div 4 = 6$
26. $7 \times 10 = 70$ $70 \div 7 = 10$
    $10 \times 7 = 70$ $70 \div 10 = 7$
27. $8 \times 5 = 40$ $40 \div 8 = 5$
    $5 \times 8 = 40$ $40 \div 5 = 8$
28. $3 \times 4 = 12$ $12 \div 3 = 4$
    $4 \times 3 = 12$ $12 \div 4 = 3$

29.

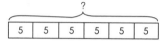

$6 \times 5 = 30$
There are **30** apples altogether.

30.

$8 \times \$10 = \$80$
Sam spends **\$80** in 8 weeks.

31.

$4 \times \$7 = \$28$
Leyla spent **\$28** altogether.

32.

$15 \div 3 = 5$
There are **5** buttons on each shirt.

33.

$100 \div 10 = 10$
Alicia needs **10** bags.

34.

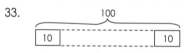

$10 \times \$5 = \$50$
Maggy will save **\$50** in 10 months.

Unit 7: Fun With Models (Multiplying and Dividing)

1.

$5 \times 10 = 50$
There are **50** stamps in all.

Singapore Math Practice Level 2A

2.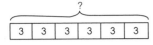

6 × 3 = 18
There are **18** eggs in 6 bags.

3.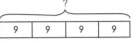

30 ÷ 5 = 6
Each of them has **6** oranges.

4.

4 × 9 = 36
He buys **36** stickers.

5.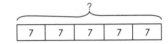

18 ÷ 2 = 9
There were **9** sunflowers in each vase.

6.

36 ÷ 4 = 9
Ms. Drew gave the markers to **9** children.

7.
7 7 7 7 7

5 × 7 = 35
5 children have **35** library books.

8.
3 3

21 ÷ 3 = 7
She used **7** plates.

Review 3

1.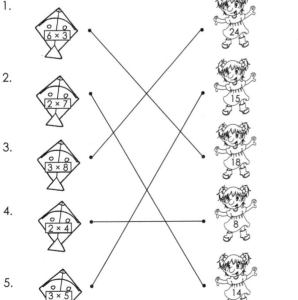
2.
3.
4.
5.

6. **8**
7. **9**
8. **6**
9. **8**
10. **7**
11. **4**
12. **2**
13. **3**
14. **5**
15. **10**
16.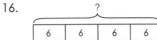

4 × 6 = 24
There are **24** pencils in 4 boxes.

17.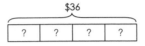

$36 ÷ 4 = $9
Each of them received **$9**.

18.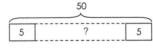

50 ÷ 5 = 10
Dad gives the muffins to **10** friends.

19.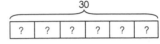

30 ÷ 6 = 5
There are **5** pieces of each color.

20.
2 2 2 2

4 × 2 = 8
She buys **8** gloves.

Unit 8: Length

1. **more**
2. **less**
3. **less**
4. **more**
5. **less**
6. (a) **A**
   (b) **B**
   (c) 4 yd. – 2 yd. = **2** yd.
   (d) 6 yd. – 4 yd. = **2** yd.
   (e) 6 yd. – 4 yd. = **2** yd.
   (f) 6 yd. – 2 yd. = **4** yd.
7. (a) **C**
   (b) **B**
   (c) 5 m – 3 m = **2** m
   (d) 3 m – 1 m = **2** m
   (e) 5 m – 1 m = **4** m
   (f) 5 m – 3 m = **2** m
8. *Lines should be the appropiate lengths and labeled correctly.*
9. *Lines should be the appropiate lengths and labeled correctly.*

115

Singapore Math Practice Level 2A

10. *Lines should be the appropiate lengths and labeled correctly.*
11. **5**
12. **3**
13. **4**
14. **2**
15. **longer than**
16. **longer than**
17. **shorter than**
18. (a) 9 cm – 2 cm = **7** cm
    (b) 13 cm – 10 cm = **3** cm
    (c) 11 cm – 6 cm = **5** cm
    (d) 10 cm – 0 cm = **10** cm
    (e) 10 cm – 3 cm = **7** cm
    (f) 7 cm – 5 cm = **2** cm
    (g) **pencil**
    (h) **eraser**
19. (a) 8 in. – 0 in. = **8** in.
    (b) 5 in. – 0 in. = **5** in.
    (c) 12 in. – 0 in. = **12** in.
    (d) 9 in. – 0 in. = **9** in.
    (e) **C**
    (f) **B**
    (g) 12 in. – 8 in. = **4** in.
    (h) **C**
        9 in. + 3 in. = 12 in.

20. **116**
$$\begin{array}{r} \overset{1}{}3\ 8 \\ +\ \ 7\ 8 \\ \hline 1\ 1\ 6 \end{array}$$

21. **36**
$$\begin{array}{r} \overset{0}{\cancel{1}}\ \overset{11}{\cancel{2}}\ \overset{15}{\cancel{5}} \\ -\ \ \ 8\ 9 \\ \hline 3\ 6 \end{array}$$

22. **515**
$$\begin{array}{r} \overset{1}{}\ \overset{1}{}\ \\ 2\ 3\ 6 \\ +2\ 7\ 9 \\ \hline 5\ 1\ 5 \end{array}$$

23. **150**
$$\begin{array}{r} 4\ 6\ 8 \\ -3\ 1\ 8 \\ \hline 1\ 5\ 0 \end{array}$$

24. **135**
$$\begin{array}{r} \overset{1}{}\ \overset{9}{}\ \overset{10}{} \\ \cancel{2}\ \cancel{0}\ \cancel{0} \\ -\ \ \ 6\ 5 \\ \hline 1\ 3\ 5 \end{array}$$

25. **520**
$$\begin{array}{r} \overset{1}{}\ \overset{1}{} \\ 3\ 9\ 9 \\ +1\ 2\ 1 \\ \hline 5\ 2\ 0 \end{array}$$

26.
278 + 516 = 794
The total length of curtains Miles sewed on both days was **794** in.

27.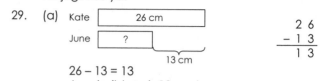
120 + 225 = 345
She travels **345** m.

28.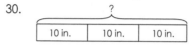
350 + 350 = 700
He jogs **700** yd.

29. (a)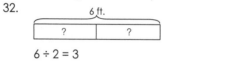
26 – 13 = 13
June's ribbon is **13** cm long.

    (b)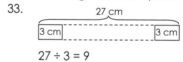
26 + 13 = 39
The total length of the 2 ribbons is **39** cm long.

30.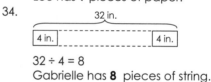
3 × 10 = 30
The length of the 3 boxes was **30** in.

31.
| 5 cm | 5 cm | 5 cm | 5 cm | 5 cm | 5 cm | 5 cm | 5 cm |
8 × 5 = 40
The length of 8 toothpicks was **40** cm.

32.
6 ft.
| ? | ? |
6 ÷ 2 = 3
The length of each piece of rope is **3** ft.

33.
27 cm
| 3 cm | | 3 cm |
27 ÷ 3 = 9
Leo has **9** pieces of paper.

34.
32 in.
| 4 in. | | 4 in. |
32 ÷ 4 = 8
Gabrielle has **8** pieces of string.

Unit 9: Mass

1. **less than**
   The toy ship rises on the balance, so it is lighter.
2. **more than**
   The camera sinks on the balance, so it is heavier.
3. **less than**
4. **more than**
5. **more than**
6. **3**
7. **45**
8. **6**
9. **4**
10. **6**
11. (a) **4**
    (b) **5**
    (c) **2**

Singapore Math Practice Level 2A

(d) bunch of bananas
(e) pineapple
(f) bunch of bananas, watermelon, pineapple
12. (a) **171**
(b) **135**
(c) **38**
(d) **Anne**
(e) **Alan**
(f) **Anne, Susan, Alan**
13. **4**
14. **6**
15. **20**
16. **9**
17. **19**
18. **200 g**
19. **450 g**
20. **50 g**
21. **380 g**
22. 500 g – 300 g = **200 g**
23. 30 lb. – 10 lb. = **20 lb.**
24. (a) 20 oz. + 20 oz. = **40 oz.**
(b) 10 oz. + 10 oz. = **20 oz.**
(c) 40 oz. – 20 oz. = **20 oz.**
25. (a) **200 g**
(b) **500 g**
(c) 500 – 200 = **300 g**
26. (b) **35 oz.**

```
    2 0
  + 1 5
    3 5
```

(c) **610 g**

```
    1
  3 6 0
+ 2 5 0
  6 1 0
```

(d) **530 lb.**

```
    1
  1 7 0
+ 3 6 0
  5 3 0
```

(e) **650 kg**

```
    1
  4 1 5
+ 2 3 5
  6 5 0
```

(f) **646 lb.**

```
    1
  5 0 9
+ 1 3 7
  6 4 6
```

(g) **861 g**

```
    1
  8 1 6
+   4 5
  8 6 1
```

HAMSTER

27. (a) **353 oz.**

```
  5 8 5
- 2 3 2
  3 5 3
```

(b) **309 g**

```
    0 16
  6 1̸ 6̸
- 3 0 7
  3 0 9
```

(c) **450 lb.**

```
  8 10
  9̸ 0̸ 0
- 4 5 0
  4 5 0
```

(d) **189 kg**

```
  2 16
  3̸ 6̸ 9
- 1 8 0
  1 8 9
```

(e) **199 lb.**

```
  7 12 18
  8̸ 3̸ 8̸
- 6 3 9
  1 9 9
```

(f) **115 g**

```
    1 10
  6 2̸ 0
- 5 0 5
  1 1 5
```

(g) **149 oz.**

```
  1 13 16
  2̸ 4̸ 6̸
-   9 7
  1 4 9
```

PUZZLES

28.

50 + 14 + 13 = 77
She uses **77** kg of ingredients altogether.

```
  5 0      6 4
+ 1 4    + 1 3
  6 4      7 7
```

29.

43 + 10 = 53
Tom's mass is **53** lb.

```
  4 3
+ 1 0
  5 3
```

30.

83 – 27 = 56
He uses **56** kg of cement.

```
  7 13
  8̸ 3̸
- 2 7
  5 6
```

31.

13 – 4 = 9
Noah's family eats **9** oz. of rice every week.

32.

945 – 380 = 565
She bought **565** g of fish.

```
  8 14
  9̸ 4̸ 5
- 3 8 0
  5 6 5
```

33.

3 × 2 lb. = 6 lb.
The total mass of the 3 bags of tomatoes was **6** lb.

34.

20 ÷ 5 = 4
Colin bought **4** bags of flour.

35.

10 × 4 = 40
The total mass of the 10 plums is **40** oz.

36.

12 ÷ 4 = 3
The mass of each bag of strawberries was **3** kg.

Singapore Math Practice Level 2A

Review 4

1. (a) 6 cm – 1 cm = **5** cm
   (b) 10 cm – 1 cm = **9** cm
   (c) 12 cm – 1 cm = **11** cm
   (d) 3 cm – 1 cm = **2** cm
   (e) 11 cm – 9 cm = **2** cm
   (f) 5 cm – 2 cm = **3** cm
   (g) 5 cm + 11 cm = **16** cm
   (h) **rubber band, hair clip, ribbon, comb**
2. **2**
3. **A**
4. **400**
5. (a) 6 cm – 1 cm = **5** cm
   (b) 11 cm – 1 cm = **10** cm
   (c) 8 cm – 1 cm = **7** cm
   (d) 8 cm – 1 cm = **7** cm
   (e) 7 cm – 5 cm = **2** cm
   (f) 10 cm – 7 cm = **3** cm
   (g) **spoon, fork**
   (h) **paintbrush, spoon, fork, key /
       paintbrush, fork, spoon, key**
6. **17**
7. (a) **3**
   (b) **4**
   (c) **2**
   (d) **toy plane**
   (e) **toy ship**
8. **C**
9. **more than**
   The bag of rice sinks on the balance. This shows that the bag of rice is heavier.
10. **less than**
    The purse rises on the balance. This shows that the purse is lighter.
11. **108**
```
    4 0
  + 6 8
  1 0 8
```
12. **356**
```
  3 1215
  4 3 5
  −   7 9
  3 5 6
```
13. **289**
```
  5 1016
  6 1 6
  − 3 2 7
  2 8 9
```
14. **350**
```
    1
  1 2 5
  + 2 2 5
  3 5 0
```
15. **772**
```
    1
  6 0 9
  + 1 6 3
  7 7 2
```
16.
```
| 525 m |
| 360 m |        ?
```
525 – 360 = 165
```
  4 12
  5 2 5
  − 3 6 0
  1 6 5
```
David's house is **165** m farther from the shopping complex than from the supermarket.

17.
```
        ?
| 375 yd. | 425 yd. |
```
```
  1 1
  3 7 5
  + 4 2 5
  8 0 0
```

375 + 425 = 800
Amanda jogs **800** yd. from her house to the stadium.

18.
```
        ?
| 8 lb. | 8 lb. |
```
2 × 8 = 16
The total mass of her luggage was **16** lb.

19.
```
          15 g
| 3 g |  --------  | 3 g |
```
15 ÷ 3 = 5
He bought **5** cherries.

20.
```
                 ?
| 10 cm | 10 cm | 10 cm | 10 cm | 10 cm |
```
5 × 10 = 50
The length of the 5 rulers was **50** cm.

Final Review

1. (a) 11 – 3 = **8** in.
   (b) 7 – 2 = **5** in.
   (c) 11 – 2 = **9** in.
   (d) 15 – 5 = **10** in.
   (e) A = 8 – 1 = **7** in.
       7 + 5 = **12** in.
   (f) **E, D, B, A, C**
2. **18**
3. **six hundred and forty-seven**
4. **303, 330, 405, 415, 540**
5. 3 × 9 = **27**
6. 237 + 508 = **745**
```
      1
    2 3 7
  + 5 0 8
    7 4 5
```
7. 717 – 169 = **548**
```
  6 1017
  7 1 7
  − 1 6 9
    5 4 8
```
8. 10 + 590 = **600**
9. 120 + 10 = **130**
10. **6 × 2 = 12**   **12 ÷ 6 = 2**
    2 × 6 = 12   **12 ÷ 2 = 6**
11. **680, 740**
    720 – 700 = 20
    660 + 20 = 680
    720 + 20 = 740
12. **4, 6, 6**

13. (a) **173 cm**
```
      1
    1 0 5
  +   6 8
    1 7 3
```
    (b) **16 lb.**
```
    2 12
    3 2
  −   1 6
      1 6
```
    (c) **8 × 3 = 24**

(d) **870**

$$
\begin{array}{r}
{}^{1}\ \ \ \\
6\ 1\ 2 \\
+\ 2\ 5\ 8 \\
\hline
8\ 7\ 0
\end{array}
$$

(e) **175**

$$
\begin{array}{r}
2\ 9\ 10 \\
\not3\ \not0\ \not0 \\
-\ 1\ 2\ 5 \\
\hline
1\ 7\ 5
\end{array}
$$

14. (a) **83 fewer yellow roses**
280 − 197 = 83

$$
\begin{array}{r}
1\ 17\ 10 \\
\not2\ \not8\ \not0 \\
-\ 1\ 9\ 7 \\
\hline
8\ 3
\end{array}
$$

(b) **595 red and white roses**
315 + 280 = 595

$$
\begin{array}{r}
3\ 1\ 5 \\
+\ 2\ 8\ 0 \\
\hline
5\ 9\ 5
\end{array}
$$

15. **$16**

$65 − $49 = $16

$$
\begin{array}{r}
5\ 15 \\
\not6\ \not5 \\
-\ 4\ 9 \\
\hline
1\ 6
\end{array}
$$

16. **460 cm of cloth**
185 + 275 = 460

$$
\begin{array}{r}
1\ \ 1 \\
1\ 8\ 5 \\
+\ 2\ 7\ 5 \\
\hline
4\ 6\ 0
\end{array}
$$

17. **7 cards**
35 ÷ 5 = 7

18. (a) **310 dog biscuits**
460 − 150 = 310

$$
\begin{array}{r}
4\ 6\ 0 \\
-\ 1\ 5\ 0 \\
\hline
3\ 1\ 0
\end{array}
$$

(b) **770 dog biscuits**
460 + 310 = 770

$$
\begin{array}{r}
4\ 6\ 0 \\
+\ 3\ 1\ 0 \\
\hline
7\ 7\ 0
\end{array}
$$

19. **21 cacti**
3 × 7 = 21

20. **330 yd.**
150 yd. + 180 yd. = 330 yd.

$$
\begin{array}{r}
{}^{1}\ \ \ \\
1\ 5\ 0 \\
+\ 1\ 8\ 0 \\
\hline
3\ 3\ 0
\end{array}
$$

21.
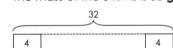

5 × 10 = 50
The mass of the 5 kiwis is **50 g**.

22.
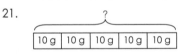

32 ÷ 4 = 8
Mrs. Coleman collected the pages from **8** students.

23.

5 × $2 = $10
She receives **$10** from Monday to Friday.

24.
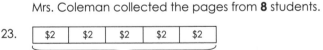

9 ÷ 3 = 3
The length of cloth received by each girl was **3 yd.**

25.
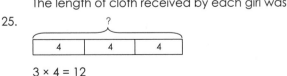

3 × 4 = 12
He needs **12 days** to make 3 bookshelves.

Challenge Questions

1. first digit: ⑧ or 9
second digit: 0, ①, 2, 3, 4, 5 or 6
third digit: 8 − 1 = 7
The 3-digit number is **817**.

2. Use the guess-and-check method.

Guess	$50	$10	$5	$1	Total
1	1	6	3	1	$126
2	1	7	1	1	$126

He used **one $50 bill, seven $10 bills, one $5 bill, and one $1 bill** to pay for the skateboard.

3.
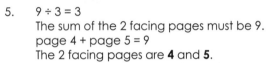

2 × 6 = 12
Jessica has **12** apples.

4. 0 1 2 ③ 4 5 6 7 8 ⑨
9 is 3 times 3.
Both are odd numbers.
Mr. Schneider's mass is **93 kg**.

5. 9 ÷ 3 = 3
The sum of the 2 facing pages must be 9.
page 4 + page 5 = 9
The 2 facing pages are **4** and **5**.

6.
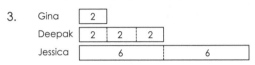

Carlos has the shortest ruler.

7.
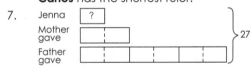

27 ÷ 9 = 3
She had **3** marbles in the beginning.

8. $100 − $20 = $80
$80 ÷ 4 = $20
He would receive four $20 bills.
Simon had one **$100 bill** in the beginning.

9. 2 + 3 + 4 = 9
The 3 numbers are **2**, **3**, and **4**.

10. 3 × 7 = 21
The sum of the 2 facing pages is 21.
page 10 + page 11 = 21
The 2 facing pages are **10** and **11**.

11.
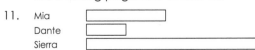

Sierra is the heaviest among the 3 children.

Singapore Math Practice Level 2A

Notes

Notes

Singapore Math Practice Level 2A

Notes

Notes

Notes

Notes

Singapore Math Practice Level 2A

Notes

Singapore Math Practice Level 2A

Notes

Singapore Math Practice Level 2A

Notes

Singapore Math Practice Level 2A